WHITE
CHINA

WHITE CHINA

*Finding the Divine
in the
Everyday*

MOLLY WOLF

Foreword by Phyllis Tickle

JOSSEY-BASS
A Wiley Imprint
www.josseybass.com

Published by Jossey-Bass

A Wiley Imprint

989 Market Street, San Francisco, CA 94103-1741   www.josseybass.com

Jossey-Bass books and products are available through most bookstores. To contact Jossey-Bass directly call our Customer Care Department within the U.S. at 800-956-7739, outside the U.S. at 317-572-3986, or fax 317-572-4002.

Jossey-Bass also publishes its books in a variety of electronic formats. Some content that appears in print may not be available in electronic books.

Unless otherwise noted, Scripture is taken from the New Revised Standard Version Bible, copyright 1989, Division of Christian Education of the National Council of the Churches of Christ in the United States of America. Used by permission. All rights reserved.

Library of Congress Cataloging-in-Publication Data

Wolf, Molly.

White China: finding the Divine in the everyday / Molly Wolf; foreword by Phyllis Tickle.

p. cm.

Includes bibliographical references.

ISBN 0–7879–6580–4 (alk. paper)

1. Christian life. I. Title.

BV4501.3.W65 2005

242—dc22   2004026726

Printed in the United States of America

FIRST EDITION

HB Printing   10 9 8 7 6 5 4 3 2 1

Contents

Contents

✤

Contents

꧁꧂

Foreword

Molly Wolf. Molly with a *y* and Wolf without an *e*. I love contradictions, and as a result I loved the woman's name before I ever began, some four or five years ago now, to read her.

Molly—it sounds round and unpretentious to me, but very substantial. Generous and solid. Someone who can be trusted to do the wise and comely thing. As names go, it smells of warm kitchens and clean barn floors and sunlight everywhere, especially sunlit wash on a line in the backyard and wide, wooden porches lush with baskets and pots of growing things—flowers and ferns and vining ivies.

But Wolf, on the other hand. . . .

Wolf is long and lean and predatory, ever on the prowl for the small, the quick, the productively elusive. Wolf is never content, is ever roaming and ever probing beyond all caution or concern for self-preservation. Wolf will dare anything, for wolf is a watchdog to Nature's order, an expedient hunter, a leader in times of winter.

Put them together, these two? Why, together, Molly and Wolf are an irreconcilable paradox caught in a powerful name. So is the woman. She validates the bit of folk wisdom holding that each of us bears the name that best describes us, while at one and the same time each of us grows to fill the name that has been given us. Molly Wolf has done this well.

The book you have in your hand, *White China,* is a compilation of pieces of Molly Wolf. One normally says that pieces are by an author; but I mean what I say. These are pieces of Molly Wolf that are as fearlessly presented and as lacking in self-protection as is the latter half of her name. No one is blocked from entering here, no one is going to be conned, and no one need hold up his or her guard while inside these pages. This is a conversation with Molly played out by the rules of Wolf.

This set of circumstances will not come as any surprise to the hundreds of people who have learned to expect just such fiercely pastoral engagement every seventh day. A Canadian for more than thirty years, Molly Wolf has been publishing "Sabbath Blessings" on both sides of the U.S.-Canadian border long enough for there to have already been several books' worth. Over the years of weekly benediction upon those who read her in whatever medium, she has grown and turned and mellowed and then abruptly charged off again, capturing at every week's turn the essence of the week's experience for those who would dare the Christian life with her and on her terms.

Molly Wolf's terms, by the way, are distinctly and unabashedly Anglican, a fact that no doubt further endears her writing to me. Historically, we Anglicans are always inclined toward those who track our Lord through the deep forests and stony places of life as well as across its meadows. This woman is a consummate tracker, and in *White China* she has bagged her best compilation to date.

Canada's verdure and Ontario's grandeur are captured here; so are the ache of a failed marriage and the anger of betrayal. The overflowing stands of flowers are here, as is the kindly, maternal voice that has labored and consistently loved the consequences, if not the pain. There is a pervasive gentleness here, made all the more acceptable by the barbed presence of reality used in its packaging. Mainly there is faith here . . . not a banquet of consolation and satiety, but just enough provender for now. Molly trusts, you see, but the Wolf hunts. This is the contradiction, but it's one a person can bank on and learn from. I suspect as well that it is what keeps so many of us coming back for more.

Phyllis Tickle
The Farm In Lucy
Eighth week of Ordinary Time, 2004

This book is in memory of my parents,
Frederick Barton Wolf, priest of the
Protestant Episcopal Church and Bishop of Maine;
and Barbara Buckley Wolf, teacher and theologian. Their souls
are in God's hand; God has brought them home,
healed them, freed them from their burdens,
and shown them mercy, true justice, love, and forgiveness.
May they rest in peace and rise in glory.

Acknowledgments

My thanks, as always, to those who sustain me. Blessings on my sons, Ross and John Greenough; on my daughters-in-the-spirit, Georgiana, Brianne, and Margaret; and on my friends, especially Deb, Anne, Mieke, T. R., Susan, Virginia, Cathy, and the Rivendell Community.

I thank the cybercommunity that upholds me day by day and preserves my sanity, and most especially the Rev. Raewynne Whiteley, who gave sage peer review. I thank God for my parish, St. James in Kingston, Ontario; Frs. Bob and Don; and my beloved choir.

I owe particular thanks to three women: Linda Roghaar, my agent; Mary Elizabeth Mason, my healer, who told me to keep on writing when I thought I couldn't; and my editor at Jossey-Bass, Sheryl Fullerton, who showed exemplary patience and faith in me. Thanks too to Andrea Flint and all the others at Jossey-Bass.

Introduction

❧

Almighty God,
to you all hearts are open,
all desires known,
and from you no secrets are hidden.
Cleanse the thoughts of our hearts
by the inspiration of your Holy Spirit,
that we may perfectly love you,
and worthily magnify your holy name;
through Christ our Lord. Amen.

—THE BOOK OF ALTERNATIVE SERVICES
OF THE ANGLICAN CHURCH OF CANADA

The coefficients of a balanced equation represent the
relative numbers of moles and reactants.

—MASTERON AND SLOWINSKI,
CHEMICAL PRINCIPLES USING THE
INTERNATIONAL SYSTEM OF UNITS

In writing about spirituality and faith, as in writing about chemistry, the real problem is one of translation. Both of the statements quoted on the previous page are synopses of reality, but somehow for nonspecialists the synopsis has come untied from the reality; because we don't understand the words, they are detached from what they represent and float off like the helium balloon of a three-year-old who has failed to hang on to the string. The three-year-old is apt to burst into wails, while we're more likely to say "Huh?" and then walk away, feeling inadequate.

The chemistry statement, if you know chemistry at all, is actually quite straightforward. It's really no different from doubling a cake recipe: if you're using four cups of flour instead of two, you need six eggs instead of three and you'll fill four eight-inch circular pans instead of two. However dressy or obscure the language, the reality is at least extremely straightforward. If you have four nitrogen atoms when you start your reaction, you're going to have four nitrogen atoms when you finish, and you're going to have to juggle all the other numbers to make that happen.

But the prayer—it's the opening to the service of the Holy Eucharist—brims with meaning, meaning tamped down almost to bursting and compressed like a bale of peat moss. This is generally the problem with God-Talk (more formidably known as theology): there is almost too much stuff packed into certain words and concepts. The core ideas go back a couple of millennia now; we've struggled with them and argued about them and sometimes even killed for them, for a very long time. But all too often, we've lost sight of what the language is actually trying to represent—a particular problem when we fall in love with the beauty of the language itself, as is fatally easy to do when the language is as beautiful as God-Talk can be.

Like chemists, those in the God-Talk business represent what they're doing with long majestic words, terms like "hermeneutics" and "soteriology" and "eschatology." The in-people can toss these terms around with understanding and aplomb, just as chemists are comfortable with words such as "stoichiometry." But this language leaves everyone who's not already in the know itching and vaguely uneasy, struggling with delusions of inadequacy or irrelevance: "Yes, but what does it all *mean*?"

White China is my personal shorthand for language like this. Untranslated words like "hermeneutics" are featureless, slippery, without life or color or realism; just as the word "coefficients" eludes your grasp unless you already know what it means. Language like this leaves you struggling in a landscape of abstraction and purity, intimidated and unsure of yourself. You don't feel comfortable handling the word. You might mispronounce it or use it wrongly, and then what would people think of you? It's a piece of pure white china, and you don't feel comfortable handling it. You might get it dirty. You might drop it and break it. It certainly can't feed you; who can eat china?

But if you take the concept or word and lay it out in the light, it all starts to makes perfect sense. *Hermeneutics* (if you're curious) means the whole set of assumptions and choices that determines what you're going to make of the Bible. Are you going to take this stuff as literal truth, or as poetic truth, and why? What dish are you bringing to this particular potluck, and why did you choose it? If you assume, for example, that the King James Version is somehow holier than any other translation, why do you make that assumption? What personal prejudices and cultural themes color the way you read a particular passage, when it could be read some other way? Why do you take this passage seriously and shrug off that one? What meaning do you give to this verse or that, and why? What do the experts have to say about the original Hebrew or Greek? What's the context? It's a great "unpacking" word, this term "hermeneutics."

Unpacking is what this book is about. I started with a small white china figurine of Christ's mother, Mary, and when I unpacked her she turned into someone who was not in the least small or white or china, but a big, warm, vibrant, earthy, real, passionate, *alive* person, one who is my sister in the skin. Then her choice to say "yes" to God became something intensely up close and personal to me. That, I believe, is what good God-Talk is about: unpacking terms and concepts and making them real. It's making the rubber hit the road. That, I hope, is what these essays do. Certainly it was my intention in writing them.

As a writer, I am madly in love with good metaphors, and I have little compunction about throwing lots of them around. Recently, an old and beloved friend handed me a real beauty that I can't resist using. My friend thinks he might have gotten it from Garrison Keillor. Bad preaching, the metaphor goes, is "putting the hay where the goats can't get it." This is not a comment about the neediness or stupidity of goats; it's a comment on poorly presented writing and speaking about God-Stuff. It's also a reminder of the duty of all of us who write or preach about Christianity: our job ultimately is to shift that bale, slice that binder twine, lay it all out, and spread out the feed so that those who hunger can eat. This can make a person feel big and important and superior, and that is the danger. But that's when we need to be humbled. We on the hay-providing side always have to remember that one person's experience is not the same as another's and my job is not to shove the hay down your throat. Above all, we hay-bale handlers have to remember, always, the warning given by our forefather in bale-handling, Paul, who said to the people of Corinth that the foolishness of God is wiser than the best wisdom of human beings. Too true.

I have no idea who you are, you who've picked up this book of mine and are looking at it now. I don't know if you, like me, are a committed Christian of the Anglican/Episcopalian stripe; maybe you are, but likely you aren't. Maybe you're a committed Christian of some other denomination. Maybe you're someone who's struggling with commitment to Christianity; I'm there too, a lot of the time. You will find major doubt in these pages. Maybe you're an agnostic or an inquirer or a would-be Wiccan. I have no way of knowing. I wish I could speak to you directly, soul-to-soul, but we aren't in the same room together over a cup of coffee. Not literally, anyway.

I don't know who you are, and I have no right to tell you what or how to believe. All I can do is to show you how I struggle with belief—and I struggle a great deal. Maybe that will keep you company in your own struggles. That's the best I can I hope for.

A note on landscapes: At the beginning of 2003, I moved from a small town south of Ottawa, Ontario, where I'd lived for sixteen years and raised my kids, to Kingston, Ontario, a small, old, beautiful, sometimes funky city at the eastern end of Lake Ontario. Some of these pieces are set in the old landscape, others in the new. All were written in a time of great transition.

Above all, enjoy.

WHITE
CHINA

—

CHAPTER 1

Creation

For every wild animal of the
forest is mine, the cattle
on a thousand hills.
I know all the birds of the air,
and all that moves in the
field is mine.
—PSALM 50:10–11

❧ One Loud, Heroic Frog ❧

Of all the (rapidly counting on fingers) eight Internet e-mail lists that I have belonged to, perhaps the most deeply eccentric was the Eastern Ontario Biodiversity Museum (EOBM) mailing list. Its members reported, sometimes a bit obsessively, whatever they were sighting in the neighborhood—which species had been seen doing what comes naturally: reports of deer in a meadow near Spencerville or a mourning cloak butterfly in somebody's backyard; queries about overwintering larvae; stories of an unsuccessful search for pickerel spawning upcreek; sightings of robins or the flight of geese.

There was one post I particularly loved: "Oxford Station, Co. Rd. 20, 3–500 m east of Smith Road turnoff, small pond on north side of county road. One loud, heroic Chorus frog calling." Now, *that's* a proper valuation. We don't take anywhere near as much delight as we should in the loud heroism of chorus frogs, dammit.

I try to be good and ecologically responsible. At migratory seasons, I still do my best to avoid those roads the frogs have to cross to get to their spawning grounds. There's always a frog massacre along certain stretches of county road when this happens— tiny sickening "thunks" from under the car wheels, and dozens of small, squashed, leg-splayed corpses on the asphalt. But although I try as much as possible to avoid involuntary amphibicide, EOBM members were out there actually counting and measuring the poor flattened bodies ("female, tibia 34.5 mm"), checking what frogs had last eaten, and mourning the deaths. To them, frogs *matter.* They worried about the implications for the future. Will this species still be with us in twenty years' time?

I keep thinking I love Nature, and I do delve into the world around me for material to write about, but I know *real* love when I see it, and I confess that compared to the EOBMers all I could manage for this landscape is a certain mild, ill-informed affection. The EOBM people were true lovers. That's what made their posts, however dotty, such a pleasure: all that love percolating through the electrons on my screen. They'd report in perfectly horrible weather, examining the fields and scrub woods and ditches, looking for things I don't think I could ever begin to notice. They'd scoop up dead fluff from the banks of creeks, probing for tiny land snails (numbers and types). Their care and knowledge gently surrounded the turtles, both painted and snapping. They'd monitor the redwing blackbirds. They'd troll the landscape for larvae and search the authorities for the information to identify their finds. They'd map what had turned up, and where. They'd watch the spread of the new, beautiful, extremely aggressive reeds that now form predatory stands along the superhighway. They'd mourn the roadkill. They'd monitor not just the arrival of the geese—we all do that!—but how many and where they're settling down for the night on their way north. They kept reporting, and every single report reminded me of love.

I don't know if I'm willing to declare absolutely that "all love creates good in some way" or that "real love is in the small stuff" but that's my experience. Maybe these things are universally true; maybe not. Maybe there are naturalists out there who are simply obsessive-compulsive cranks; if so, I haven't met any yet. Obsessive-compulsive crankiness does not leak from that post about that "loud, heroic Chorus frog." I think naturalists do what I do—which is simply to love Creation because Creation is so very lovable—but they know how to do it properly: in detail, and in knowledge gained from genuine care and deep interest.

Can Creation feel this love, somehow? I can't imagine how it could, but I know that my imagination often falls far short of possible realities. I gather that at least some of these naturalists don't feel any need to find God in all this, and that's fine with me. But I do believe in a Creator, and I can imagine a Creator who is deeply pleased by the fact that somebody's *noticing* all those land snails. I too create stuff, and I know that having my creations noticed with pleasure is a wonderful feeling. It's not why I do the creating, of course, but it's one of those side-pleasures, like finding a twenty-dollar bill in your raincoat pocket.

I don't think I'd care, honestly, if Creation turns out to be as contingent as some scientists believe—if it's all one big, happy accident. Strangely, it wouldn't bother me one bit to be proved wrong about God's action as Creator, because if I'm wrong there's probably some sort of mystery behind the wrongness, and nothing is more fun, more deeply pleasing, than mystery—the great swirling deep blue shot with silver. God can be whatever God damn well pleases, and Creation is as Creation is. Though most of us do believe that God includes Creator, if we're wrong, we'll get over it. In the meantime, there's still Creation, which is well worth loving for its own sake.

But there is a sort of glory in Creation that I'd sooner ascribe to God than to accident. Not a glory in Neiman Marcus terms; not a matter of Renaissance angels in terribly good taste. You can't live in this landscape, especially in spring mud season, without losing any illusions about the niceness, cuteness, and prettiness of Creation. After all, early spring is the only time of year when we can have both snow *and* the very earliest mosquitoes.

No, if there's any glory around here, it's in the rich abundance and profound relatedness of all sorts of ecosystems great and small, from the senile pine plantings to the cedar swamps, from abandoned meadows succumbing to alder and sumac to the banks of creeks and rivers. There are a gazillion species out there, each with its own particular characteristics and its own particular place in this small part of the world, and that is indeed enough glory for any reasonable human being. Maybe it's all pure accident, mere coincidence, but some of us do tend to believe that coincidence is God staying anonymous.

What does hold, though, is that if you want to think of God as Creator, if you want to sink your spiritual toes deep into the richness of Incarnation, then reading a whole lot of e-mail reports from rural naturalists in Eastern Ontario in spring mud season is a fruitful use of your time. It keeps you humble, for starters; it keeps you rooted (sorry!). It keeps you from lapsing into besotted musings on the Beeyootiful Rrrromance of Nature. It reminds you that we less-than-angels have been much, much less than angelic in our treatment of the world that sustains and upholds us. It nudges you to recollect that however bleak, sodden, and unlovable this world sometimes looks, there are still any number of fascinating, hopeful details, if you're willing to take a close look at what's right under your foot (not, one hopes, a loud, heroic chorus frog).

What I do believe for myself is that God surrounds each bit of God's Creation with the same detailed, particular, loving attention that the EOBMers have for the creatures they monitor. I believe this love extends from individual ant (or even smaller) to galaxy. It is the warm, delighted look of a mother bending to her newborn child, not because the child has done anything to earn this love, but simply because the child *is*.

I am too painfully aware of the arrogance of humankind to be comfortable saying that we matter more to God than (say) porpoises; I believe that God takes enormous delight in the porpoisefulness of porpoises. But I also believe that God entered into this Creation in the person of a human being, Jesus the Christ, because we have particular capabilities that are (as best we know) unique to being human. Perhaps God self-manifests to land snails in another dimension; not being a land snail, I have no way of knowing.

But I do know what the scent of true love smells like, and I could feel it coming in from these people, trolling through Creation and noticing it, treasuring it, recording it, in depth and detail—turning Creation over in the palm of the hand as a jeweler examines a prized pearl.

Me, I'm just sitting here, humbly waiting for the herons.

❧ Chocolate ❧

It is February; the days, blessedly, are growing longer, and we have exchanged the brutal, bitter brilliance of high winter for the mush and muddle of low winter. For the last few days, what's been coming down from the sky hasn't been real snow, but something closer to virginal slush—snow so wet and heavy that lifting a shovelful is nearly dangerous. There's been a lot of it, too.

I have to say one thing for a city with a world-class university: you wouldn't believe the sophistication of some of the student-built snowpersons over in the Queen's Ghetto (the student part of town). Male and female they created them, yes indeed, some of them very male and female indeed. I suppose that's the gift of wet snow; you can do real anatomical correctness with this stuff. And then there are the snow forts. One was clearly the work of engineering students. The crenellation was a nice touch.

But even with the milder weather, people hereabouts seem generally fed up with the fact of winter. We are all grousing madly. It has been going on long enough, thank you; we would like it to stop *right now.* This, alas, is rather like a woman trying to take a coffee break while she's in the middle of birthing a baby: "Look, I promise I'll get back to it in ten minutes; I just want a bit of a break." Sorry. No way.

Since a time-out is not possible, I would like to propose an amendment to the laws of nature, as follows:

In all parts of the Northern Hemisphere north of the
  forty-fifth parallel,
and in those other parts of the Northern Hemisphere
that might just as well be north of the forty-fifth parallel,
given what winter is like there,
during the month of February
chocolate shall have no calories.

I mean, God knows we *need* chocolate in weather like this; we need it to slog through the endless tail of winter just as Harry Potter needed it as anti-Dementors medication. Since it's a need, not a wish, it shouldn't carry any penalties, like weight gain, should it? Right?

Sigh.

Pure foolishness, of course. No, chocolate is not going to lose its fat-creating calories, even in February when slush is falling from the skies. Winter is going to hang on here until it's ready to go, in six weeks if we're lucky, eight or ten if we aren't. This is February; this is Great-Lake-side southern Canada. What did we expect, feathers?

It's natural, if we believe in an all-powerful God, to imagine that God could rearrange the natural order of things whenever God felt like doing so. If God set the rules, then God gets to bend them, no? That's how we'd operate if we were in control of things. What we'd do is wipe out winter, hunger, pain, oppression, all the discomforts and evils of this world.

So why doesn't God do just that?

The answer, I suppose, is that God doesn't see discomfort quite the way we do. I do not believe for a moment that God wills suffering; what God wills is our ability to bring something meaningful out of suffering. But at the same time, I do believe God does not put a particularly high value on comfort. In fact, discomfort has real grace about it, if we choose to use it creatively. I may kvetch about late winter, but the fact is that I'm really extremely comfortable by world standards, and I have chosen to live here, in this climate; it's as unreasonable for me to demand that spring come earlier as it is for me to demand that chocolate have no calories.

But I do wonder. I wonder if God, at the outset of creating Creation (however it happened), sent God's imaginative Spirit out to range freely throughout space and time, like a bird over the waters. I remember the Biblical image of the formless void, covered by darkness, over which the wind of God sweeps, searching, probing, considering, trying out possibilities: *What will happen if I do it this way?* Perhaps the mind of God considered the possibility of making sure that no toe got stubbed and no evil occurred, but God realized that this was going to require either a Creation with no real freedom or a Creation in which God would have to micromanage everyone and everything on a scale at once immeasurably grandiose and maddeningly minute. And so, good Creator that God was, God thought: *No, I don't think so.*

Or—daring thought!—it might be that God is still actively creating, because Creation (having a will of its own) doesn't always go the way God wants it to, and God and Creation are working it out together. But there's an element of jury-rigging. It doesn't always go as planned. Not exactly the traditional view, but a notion with which the front-line theologians are fooling around quite happily these days.

The old line about the problem of pain is, "If God is God, he is not good; if God is good, he is not God." That is, we can have a loving God, or we can have an all-powerful God, but we can't have both. Not given the reality of real suffering.

There is another possibility, though. It could be that we have a God who knows how it will all turn out in the very long run, and who knows that in the end (as C. S. Lewis put it in *The Great Divorce*) glory will wash backward into all Creation. This is a God whose time is not an arrow flying only forward, but something far more mysterious. Is this so difficult to imagine? We humans have time running in only one direction, forward, because that's how we experience life: cradle to grave, no turning back. For us, the angel Time stands with a sword at the gates of Eden, saying "You can't go back." We have only *chronos,* human-type time. But is God's time so necessarily limited? Could God's time, *kairos,* move back and forth freely like a bead on a string—or even perhaps like a bead in a box? If so, then what could this mean for us in Creation?

In the meantime, I cannot expect the Almighty to upset the natural order of things simply because I don't like the way they're going, a point Jesus made very clearly. When the tempter urged him to play fast and loose with the laws of gravity by jumping off the pinnacle of the Temple, Jesus responded, "I'm not going to put God to the test" (Matthew 4:5–7). I have to accept that this is the way the world I live in operates, and I can trust it to go on pretty much as it usually does because this is how my Creator made it.

What we can do, however, is make of late winter what we can, whether it's crenellated snow forts or random acts of kindness. I can haul my own grocery cart back to the store instead of leaving it for the supermarket kids, because pushing those things through slush is brutal. I can giggle over the anatomically correct snowpersons. I can enjoy the deeply satisfying *thunk* you hear when you succeed in kicking all the built-up snow crud out of your car's wheel wells—ah, poor, deprived non-winter people who don't know that one! I can refuse to be any more grouchy than absolutely necessary. I can remember that it's only February, and I do not live in Iqaluit, where spring arrives very late indeed.

We can get grouchier in late winter, more apt to take offense; we can retire to the TV or hunker down with a stack of mystery novels and let the world go to hell in a handbasket. Or we can make another choice.

We can remember that discomfort never killed a person, and in fact it can be a wonderfully teaching thing, and that discomfort is not the same as suffering. Yes, walking and driving are quite horrible, given the mushy mess—but it's no longer necessary to put your gloves back on before turning the parking meter handle. The light is growing stronger and longer. *Only six more weeks if we're lucky, ten at the max.*

Homemade bread, toasted, with the merest smear of butter and honey. The smile of a snowsuited baby enthroned in her carrier in the supermarket. Jokes about the weather called out between neighbors. The golden streetlight shining sideways through thick, lazy flakes that you can capture with the tip of your tongue. Small things. As good as chocolate, maybe better.

❧ Leaves ❧

Because of the rather peculiar weather—drought coupled with warmer-than-usual temperatures until last week—leaf season has been less than spectacular this fall. Only in the last couple of days have we seen the usual flame colors, and they're diluted by a lot of dusty green.

But the night before last we had a real, hard frost, with the usual results. My friend Anne's big gingko tree dropped every single one of its leaves in the course of two hours—floomph! The butternut tree on the side street by the supermarket likewise bombed the scenery with its fruit, to the delight of the squirrels. Suddenly there were drifts of dry leaves, unraked and unblown, that a person could scuffle through on her way to and from the store.

So a person did just that, reveling in the color and dry-taffeta rustle of them, kicking them into small showers. To the best of my knowledge—although there are decades I try not to remember in any real detail—I have done this every single year since I was a small child, except for three autumns when I lived downtown in a city, where there were no trees at all. It's going on half a century of leaf-shuffling by now. I fully intend to keep on with the practice as long as I have access to leaves and the use of my legs, and I plan to get steadily sillier and less inhibited about it in my cranky old age.

Leaf-kicking yesterday, I came away from a conversation with an old friend who confesses that he feels completely unchanged from the person he was when I first met him, when we were both eighteen. I don't feel this way at all; I hardly remember the person I was all those years ago. I'm not sure I'd recognize my old self if I met her on the street now. I am not the same person I was when, as a child, I first discovered the joys of leaf-shuffling, and God. Too much has happened since, for better and worse: I have lost some and gained much. The body turns over completely every seven years or so. Statistically speaking, I don't have a single atom in common with the person I was when I started writing God-Stuff a mere ten years ago, much less the person I was when I met this guy for the first time more than three-times-ten years ago (closer to four-times-ten, horrible thought!) or the person I was when I first learned to kick leaves five-times-ten years ago.

And yet, and yet. I carry on my forehead a scar I got when I was learning to walk. My forearms show, very faintly, the ghosts of the folds of fat on my baby arms. My sister recently gave me a photo of myself at eighteen, and that leggy girl and I use exactly the same gesture to tuck our hair behind our ears. I still shuffle through leaves every fall, without fail.

We tend to think of permanence versus change without remembering that they coexist—that we are, at one and the same time, creatures of change and constancy. I know from having had children that each child is born with a spirit unlike any other spirit, and that although much can dim or warp that spirit, nothing but death can extinguish it—and as a Christian, I'm pretty sure that the spirit survives even death.

I have kicked leaves under the same rich sky—the blue that chocolate would be if chocolate were blue—in two countries, six states, and two provinces. I have kicked leaves when my spirit bounced in joy and when it dragged as limp as a sack of wet laundry. I have kicked leaves in faith and in disbelief and (most often) in a state painfully dangling somewhere between the two. I have kicked leaves in love and anger and despair and hope. I have taught leaf-kicking to my children—funny, it's one of those things, like slurping spaghetti strands, that they don't know by instinct (or at least mine didn't). I have kicked leaves because it's a joy that I cling to with both hands and two feet, and because I know it's something you have to grab when it comes. You get that chance only once a year, and next year, who knows?

This year I am leaf-kicking with my faith in the deepest disarray. Checking it over, the way a medic might check over a carcrash victim for fractures, I find that my theology is hanging in there and that my down-deep God-certainty is still solid. But my own spirituality, my sense of meaning and trust, is in tatters. Too many Interesting Times, I suppose. Sometimes, the leaf-kicking little kid in me feels that God periodically heaves me overboard and watches me struggle in the water without lifting a finger to make it any easier.

My head and my gut know better, and they are what keep me going, but my faith-heart is so terribly tired and sore. Writing, which used to be such a joy, is somewhere between a burden and an impossibility: I find myself wanting to storm away from it, or simply abandon it as a bad job and find something that pays better and asks less. These days, about all I can do with any sureness, it seems, is simply wait.

There are those, I know, who would see this state as a failure on my part. "You just have to *believe*," they would say. "You just have to pray. Prayer always works." Maybe for them it does. But maybe that's not my vocation here, the place to which I am called. Maybe I'm supposed to be sitting with those who are hurting, who are doubting, who have tried prayer and fallen back defeated. Maybe there's supposed to be the occasional writer of God-Stuff who has problems with deep-down doubt. Maybe that's what I'm supposed to be writing—because God reaches to us where we are, not where we ought to be.

I was a child in the spirit when I started off on this journey, but I'm older now, and I see through a woman's eyes. I know that this sort of collapse is a normal part of the Great Journey. It's like mud season around here, a necessary time of preparation. These leaves will fall and be blown away, rotting back into the soil, and next spring we'll see the greenish blush high up in the trees as the leaves bud out. I know so with my head and gut, and my heart is just going to have to take it on trust.

At this season, the great Vs of geese gather and head south. I didn't know geese when I was younger; they've been a gift and a discovery of my middle age. I watch as they beat their way south, knowing that we're heading into fall mud season and another Canadian winter. I will see them come back in the spring. I know that if I trust my head and gut, my heart's faith will inevitably follow, just as the geese follow their knowledge of the rivers and landscape. It's just that sometimes it seems to take so long. So many months until the geese and the leaves come back—and of course by then, they won't be exactly the same geese, and certainly not the same leaves, and I won't be exactly who I am now, because all living things must change. The only life form that doesn't change is one that's dead.

Plus ça change, plus c'est la même chose. It's raining today, and the leaves will have lost their crispness by now. Maybe I've had all the leaf-kicking I'm going to get this year; maybe I'll luck out and get another chance. I don't know. When this time comes around in another twelve months, I'll grab my chance again. However different things may be, that always stays the same.

🍃 Maggie 🍃

Magnificat leaps effortlessly up onto my desktop, treads lightly across the keyboard (thereby totally gumming up my onscreen work), and lays one small imperious paw on my left shoulder. The rest follows almost immediately. I curve my arm up to support her, and she gives a good wiggle and settles down, purrbox revving. Ever since she was a baby, Maggie has liked to cuddle up on this particular part of my anatomy, but now that she's a half-grown cat, she occupies a lot more space than she used to.

What's still so young about her is her (apparently absolute) belief that she *owns* my left shoulder—that she's entitled by right to curl up, with my arm underneath, supporting her, whenever the spirit moves her. In fact, sometimes I don't want to hold her. I want to get on with my writing or answer my e-mail, and I am a two-handed typist. So I put her down, and she jumps up again, and I put her down, and she jumps up again. Sometimes we compromise and she curls up between me and the keyboard, which is reasonable. Sometimes she gives up and trots off to make the older cats' lives a little more miserable. But sometimes she's so persistent I have to throw her out of my office and close the door.

A sense of prerogative belongs to the young, I think. Most of us learn sooner or later, more or less painfully, that there will *always* be a pea under the mattress and that the peasantry, instead of piling on the futons to our complete satisfaction, will just stare at us and say "You expected maybe featherbeds?" We learn that life isn't going to revolve around us or give us everything we want, and we'd best get used to it and move on. The role of the princess (Maggie included) isn't to have her every desire catered to. The role of the princess is to grow up. Same goes for princes.

For some of us, it just doesn't happen. I don't know why— whether some failing of early nurturing leaves a person incapable of this sort of maturation, or whether it's the sign of an extremely strong and determined personality, or maybe both, or something else. But some of us simply refuse to give up our sense of entitlement. It's a very sad way to be, because anyone like this is going to be in for a whole lot of disappointment as the world fails to oblige. The truly determined blame everyone but themselves for this sad state of affairs: *they're* asking only for what's reasonable and for their rights, and what's everybody else's problem? Maggie knows what Maggie wants, and she sees no reason why she shouldn't get it.

Most of us, however, do learn from our disappointments. We discover that we're certainly not always going to get what we want, and sometimes we won't even get what we honestly deserve. Sometimes there ain't no justice. Of course this cuts two ways (sometimes we should be deeply relieved that we don't get what we deserve!), but the injustice, when it's not in our favor, can be very hard to take. We've done such a good job, but the promotion goes to someone else. We worked so hard at the marriage, doing everything the experts said, and it still failed. We tried so hard with the kids, and they went off the rails. We're left holding only a bag of guilt and anger and disappointment, it seems.

It doesn't occur to us that there is an even bigger injustice lurking in life, a huge insult to our sense of natural justice, one that Christ described in the parable of the vineyard workers (Matthew 20:1–16). The landowner hires workers at different times in the day, so that some put in a full day and others only an hour or so— but then he pays them all the same amount. It's a maddening parable, especially because we always figure we'd be the virtuous early birds getting the shaft, not the shiftless late ones getting the bonus. It feels so *unfair.*

The injustice is God's grace. It isn't fair, it isn't reasonable; it is a deep offense to our sense of natural justice. In fact, it sometimes drives us buggy, but there it is. God offers unconditional love and forgiveness to all, even the people we disapprove of. The only thing he asks in exchange is that we accept these gifts of grace and, by our acceptance, allow him to transform our lives. We can, of course, refuse the gift; God is an insistent lover, but he has excellent manners and doesn't force on us what we don't want to accept. He delights in our *yes* but he will respect our *no.*

The problem with our *no,* however, is that ultimately it leads to hell—not to Dante's Inferno or the younger Brueghel's grotesqueries, but to a private, personal hell of resentment and rage and disappointment as we watch God's apparent injustice unfold. Why doesn't God punish our enemies the way we want? We want them to fry in hell; we want them writhing in the torments; we want them to stand before a God who hates them just as much as we hate them, and we want to be there to watch the expression on their faces as they realize what they're in for. We want God to be just as vindictive as we are, because that would justify our resentment. It makes us the right ones, the winners.

God just won't oblige. Instead, if they want him, he's there for our enemies too, like the father in the parable of the prodigal son—running toward the one who left and then returned in shame with arms outstretched in love and longing, calling for jubilation. It's just not *fair.*

Our sense of outrage goes back to the sense of entitlement we never quite outgrow. I am good and deserving, and I want X and deserve X, and if I don't get X then there's something wrong with the world, not with me. The more we concentrate on our own rights and the other guy's wrongs (in both senses of right and wrong), the deeper we dig ourselves into the combined state of entitlement and disappointment that leads straight into those good old sins of pride and anger.

Why won't God reward us for our righteousness, as we deserve? It doesn't occur to us that maybe God doesn't want our best behavior, much less the mind-set that concentrates on being "righteous." Not one of us is up to God's standards of righteousness, after all. But God still wants *us*—"just as I am, without one plea" as the old hymn says, and he wants us most when we're shaky and vulnerable and unsure of ourselves, not when we're preening ourselves on what good people we are. He wants us in the state of utter emptied-out transparency where we see how broken we truly are, how much we've been given, and how little we've truly deserved.

Kittens are different. It is in the Maggieness of Maggie to grow from the bouncy selfishness of kittenhood to the more serene and dignified selfishness of adult cathood, because that's what cats are about. The justified cat—the cat who has become all that he or she can be—would still have that sense of entitlement because it's hardwired into the feline personality, as anyone who lives with a cat knows. It's not in Maggie's deck of cards to grow, step by step and often very painfully, into this simultaneous awareness both of our undeserving and of God's loving mercy. (I suspect that God finds cats extremely restful.)

But we are human, and our best way of being is different from Maggie's. If we are to become all God designs us to be, we have to let go of that sense of entitlement and injustice, and accept our need for mercy and grace, instead of trying to make sure that our enemies get it in the neck. God's grace is so deeply unjust it means that sinners don't get what they deserve. Thank God for that.

❦ Ducks ❦

True, Lake Ontario is the smallest of the Great Lakes, and true, my end of it is comparatively sheltered by a series of good-sized islands, but it is still quite a big body of water. Wind makes all large bodies of water rather restless. This one particular evening was a whippy one—windy enough to make the great blue heron overhead work hard in its flight; windy enough if not to kick up swells then at least to create quite a respectable chop. I was enjoying the chop as I walked the path by the water's edge, watching it slap, scour, and foam its way over weathered limestone shingle.

A couple of yards offshore, two ducks rode the choppy water serenely, bobbing up and down in perfect unison, looking as completely at home as you might feel in your best-beloved overstuffed armchair with a good book and a cup of coffee at your side. They looked the picture of duckly contentment, perhaps because their ducklings were nowhere in sight: mom and dad taking a break from the nippers. I stopped and watched them for a while, mildly jealous. They looked so quiet, so peaceable.

I had only recently come out of quite choppy waters myself. Frankly, I resented every minute I spent in them. None of this serene wave-riding for me, this contented bobbing up and down as spume foamed up at the water's edge. No, I felt that after all the tumult I'd already dealt with I'd earned a bit of peace and quiet. It's one of the fallacies of life in Interesting Times that you figure you're overdue for the good stuff, that there's some sort of balance to be had. It's the same impulse that caused someone to tack an extra-happy (and palpably made-up) ending onto the Book of Job. At first all the stresses bugged me; then they began to make me frightened and depressed—is life *always* going to be so problematic? Is this just the way it's meant to be?

I don't want to learn to ride the waves. I just want the @#$! waves to stop, and the wind to calm, and the water to be clear and peaceful with a temperature of about 82°F, give or take half a degree. I want the sun to be fine but not strong; I want a pleasant lake breeze but not too much; I want a bathing suit that looks becoming on the body I ought to have but don't. The culture in which I bob, like the ducks on their waves, tells me that I *should* have all these things—that they are my right.

Removing my gaze from my own navel and looking around, I can't help seeing people—perfectly innocent people—for whom life is not all right, has never been, probably never will be; people who suffer far more than I ever have and who *have* learned to bob along like those ducks, somehow managing, even with grace, to cope with burdens they have done nothing to deserve. People with MS or major mental illness, people still struggling with childhood abuse, people with intractable pain, people in deep mourning, people living in poverty in a society that views poverty as a moral crime. I live in a city of broken people, and it's an extremely useful corrective to my own self-pity.

I struggle always with the common problem of believers everywhere: Where is the biblical God who always answers prayer, who punishes the wicked and comforts the afflicted and rewards the good? It doesn't compute. My childish heart still demands a God who meets those expectations, even as my somewhat-less-childish head reminds me that the Kingdom hasn't fully happened yet, and it probably won't in my lifetime. This is a world still subject to the three great necessary wild cards of biology, physics, and human free will. Wherever there is greed, dishonesty, and fear (and where isn't there?), there is inevitably trouble.

As a believer, I have to take it on faith that God is working out God's purposes and sometimes, looking around, it's possible to see real progress, real signs of liberation, as we break free of constraints based on fear, prejudice, or the need to control. We are, for example, far more aware now of racism than we were when I was a child, and we see the need not to accept it but to root it out. This *is* progress. We are beginning to be more aware of our responsibilities toward this earth and all who live in it. We've seen progress in the liberation of women, and the confrontation of violence against them and against children. Incomplete as it always is, our knowledge is still deeper and richer by far than the crude old mechanistic models.

I have to remember all this. I have to keep firmly in mind that I know no more of God's purposes than those ducks do of global politics. I can't take a view as huge in time and space as God can; I can see only my own small patch of water, now ruffled, now smooth, and adapt to whatever conditions life sends me, as best I can. I must trust that, as Dame Julian of Norwich promised, in time "all will be well, and all will be well, and all manner of things will be well."

OK, God, I'll try to do it your way, and I'll trust you (gulp!) to send me whatever you know I need, even if it's not necessarily what I think I want. I do not believe that you send me suffering. I do believe that you stand with me in suffering, and that you send me the strength I need to run my life as best I can. We've done this a lot before.

It didn't occur to me to wonder, until much later, just how hard those ducks were paddling.

Bonsai

As part of a new phase in my life, I am building up a collection of house plants. I love house plants. Years ago, I tried raising them, but life being as it was back then I rarely remembered to water them and the inevitable transpired.

I managed not to kill a big spider plant—tough old thing! I bought an ivy and a peperomia to dress up the old house for sale. These three plants came with me when I moved, the last things I took out of the house where my family and I had lived for sixteen years. Now, repotted, the spider plant swung in the dining room window, doing gloriously, and I just had to repot the ivy too. They were joined by about a dozen others: a big monstera, a handsome weeping fig, a young but promising rubber plant, a jade plant (now recovering from my having left it out in bright sun for too many days), a really beautiful variegated pothos, and so forth and so on. They now get watered regularly, fed routinely, and misted daily, so they're all doing well.

Now, whenever I go to Home Depot or the grocery store, I do a small tour of the house plant section, looking for something to grab my fancy. I don't let myself get carried away; I have only two good south-facing windows and not all the space in the world. Just the other day, I managed to say no to a huge and beautiful silver-spotted dieffenbachia, with difficulty.

But what really grabs my eye at the moment is bonsai. Not for the predictable reasons, though.

I understand the appeal of bonsai trees: how they reflect, in miniature, the crabbed beauty of trees that survive against all the odds—pines that grow on rocky crests exposed to the worst of winter. Where I live, the landscape is dominated by the Canadian Shield, an immense and ancient rocky apron surrounding Hudson's Bay and stretching far down toward the Great Lakes. Our country's first modern painters fell in love with the harsh, spectacular landscape of the Shield and painted trees bent and shaped by the power of adversity. You can't help but admire trees like that, holding on, living sometimes hundreds of years, twisted and gnarled by the weather into a superb, compelling elegance—just as my deepest admiration goes to those who, in unbearable circumstances, manage to scrape together kindness, compassion and love while they are themselves suffering. It happens. This is where the beauty of poverty lies, and it is real.

Bonsai, on the other hand, don't get that way because of nature; they grow into this harsh beauty because we've chosen to do it to them. We take normal seedlings and by dint of the most skilled, meticulous artfulness shape them into something (let's face it) tiny and stunted. We do so lovingly, using the most careful pruning of leaf, twig and root, softening copper wire to reshape a branch in precisely the right direction. We force growth into the trunk, making it woody and giving it the odd artistic twist. We bend a branch to reroot to the soil. We train the whole plant to cascade like water over the side of its pot.

But is that what's right for the plant? Is this what it's intended to do? Or have we forced it to be something other than what it should be?

This greatly bothers me, not because bonsai are so important in and of themselves but because of what we do to each other. As a mother, I found I had to distinguish carefully (and didn't always manage it) between setting necessary standards and limits with my kids, on the one hand, and trying to make them into what I wanted them to be, on the other. Kids do need rules; they do need standards of appropriate conduct; they do need to have expectations made of them. No quarrel with that.

But what happens when we try to shape the child in ways that aren't right for him? What if what I think is best for her really isn't best at all? At the moment, we (well, some of us—not I, for one) are bent on forcing children, like bonsai, into a sort of hyper-competitive gotta-do-it-all, racing from piano lessons to math coach to chess tutor to competitive swimming. It's the old "bend the twig" bit—but what kind of tree are we envisaging? Do we leave room for less obviously essential purposes—play, dreaming, imagination?

I remember all too well what it's like to have your natural shape pruned and bound into something that pleases another person, whose vision of you isn't you at all, but something very different. "I love you so much that I'm going to correct everything that's wrong about you, so you'll look the way I think you should look and make me proud of you"—what does that say, really? It is at best an equivocal sort of "love"; at worst, it saws off the beloved at the ankles.

What is God's intent for us, trees or children? I used to buy into the notion of suffering as formational or ennobling—that the potter had to get rough with the clay. Now I'm not so sure. I've seen and experienced too much suffering that I cannot view as justified in any way, and I see the ensuing damage—not the beauty, but real damage. My theology is going through any number of tiny bumps and shifts these days. I am beginning to believe in a God who wants us to flourish, to grow to our greatest potential, freely, but in community—to be not bonsai but trees of the fullest, most magnificent habit. I'm still thinking about this.

I have the strangest impulse now, when I see a bonsai in Home Depot. I want to buy the plant, bring it home, strip off any wiring, pot it up into rich, light soil, keep it carefully watered and misted daily, set by a south-facing window, and see how it grows. A bonsai could never grow into the tree it might have been, not after all that pruning and wiring, but it might grow into a new beauty all its own.

I'll think about it.

✿ Tree and Fence ✿

The neighborhood where I now live is full of chain-linked fences, put up when the houses were brand new, about thirty years ago. At a guess, I'd say the fences were intended to keep kids from cutting across people's backyards to take the shortest route from A to B, as kids always will. Over time, the fences and the neighborhood have worked out certain accommodations. It's really pretty silly (pedestrians think) to have to walk three blocks out of your way when, with a stout pair of wire cutters, you could arrange things quite differently. Pragmatically, someone has put metal bars across the gaps cut in the fences so that you can't take a bicycle or motor bike through. There are only a few gaps, all of them very well used. But the fences remain.

Out walking, I noted one odd spot where a young weed tree of some sort—can't tell what type without the leaves being out—had grown up through a bit of fence. It must have started small, a seedling, then a foot-high sapling, weaving its way by accident through the steel meshes, uncorrected. Then, as its branches started to form, they too twined themselves into the fence, and the branches' branches too. Now the tree is several feet taller than the fence and inextricably woven into it. The tree's bole is now three or four inches across, and bole and branches have hardened. In some places they've grown around the wire, wrapping it into the wood. There is no way the tree and the fence can now be parted. Even if you cut down the tree, you couldn't cut the wood out of the mesh without a huge amount of work, and it just wouldn't be worth it. The only hope for the tree in this situation is that, in the long struggle between wood and wire, the tree may actually take the fence apart before someone notices, takes the tree down, and rebuilds the fence.

Sometimes it feels as though people are in the same predicament. Some accidents of nature, a few bad choices, a failure of love, and we feel as though we're as trapped in the unyielding mesh of our lives as that tree is in the fence, and with no more hope of setting things right. All we can do (we think) is carry on carrying on, doing the best we can, wrapping ourselves around each new piece of damage as the tree has wrapped itself around wire, and accepting it as patiently as we can. Our only hope is that in the fullness of time the fence into which we've grown will somehow take itself away, or that we'll grow so accustomed to it that we won't notice it anymore. But things never seem to go that way, or not predictably enough for us to have trust. We seem to be trapped, living either in pain and anger, or in the numbness and anxiety that replace pain and anger when we refuse to entertain them.

Yes, sometimes we *are* confined by chance or choice that we can't change. A diagnosis of schizophrenia, a genetic disorder, cultural expectations that we have no ability to escape, systematic poverty: these are things we may have to find a way of living with. We can struggle against them; we can understand what they mean for us, and we must certainly learn to manage as best we can. I can't look at what's happening in the Sudan in this time and speak about people making free choices; it would be an insult to those trapped by civil war.

But for most of us in our ordinary lives, the traps are different; they are things we can become conscious of, and at least potentially change.

What, in the tree and fence, could the Gospel message be? I wrote this question, and the word *repent* promptly popped into my mind. It's a loaded and deeply unpopular word, for excellent reasons. We tend to see *repent* as meaning "stop doing all that bad stuff and straighten up and fly right." But maybe it could mean something else; maybe it means something more like "it doesn't have to be like this." Maybe it is a word against entrapment and rigidity, a word about the soul's ability to soften, bend, and flow into new ways of being. Maybe it's a word about choosing plasticity over rigidity, movement over stasis.

Isn't this what Easter is about, in some way? Can there be anything more rigid and unbending than death, any situation a more certain trap than the Crucifixion? But Christ slips through death's clutching fingers, freed, shaking off the shackles and turning back into the brightness of life, as though somehow the wood of the trapped tree has turned soft again and can be teased free of the metal and set free—set to rights. God votes, it seems, for plasticity.

God votes for plasticity—but we vote for rigidity. We stay trapped in patterns that we put there in the first place (often for good reason) but retain even after they've turned destructive. Why? Often for fear or sheer habit, or a failure of hope and imagination, or anger we haven't dealt with—oh, that's a fine bit of fencing, that one! Changing how we operate looks like such hard work, and it's not what we learned in school or at home, and it's just easier to go on this way. Or we see rigidity as a good thing in and of itself, not seeing how it can trap us, not wanting to hear about the problems it causes others: "I am firm, you are stubborn, he is a pig-headed fool."

Maybe sometimes the fence is real and we truly are stuck with the thing. But looking around my personal landscape, I can't think of an example, although I can see any number of people who have chosen to freeze into patterns of rigidity that leave them trapped. Even for those whose lives are dreadfully limited by circumstances they really can't alter, there's still the choice to turn themselves Godward or turn away.

For myself, I'll vote for plasticity, for the possibility of real change—for hope, even. I will trust that wherever and whenever I feel myself trapped, I may find my way to freedom if I'm willing to choose to be soft instead of strong and to trust God instead of doing it my way. I will trust that however hard it is to see beyond my own entrapments, God has things up God's sleeve that I cannot begin to ask or imagine. I will trust that I am not like the tree in the fence; I may choose to flow in new directions, freely.

That's my choice, and I'll stick with it.

❧ Milkweed ❧

The park lies just the other side of the city's small airport, a promontory jutting out into the lake and catching the westerly wind. A good deal of it used to be farmland—usually a mistake in these parts, where the limestone lies inches beneath the soil surface. Some of it is now under maturing forest; other parts have young trees planted. It's a conservation area now, rich in birds and much loved by the people who live here.

I don't know it at all well. I think I've walked here maybe four or five times in the year or so I've lived in this city—not enough to be familiar with the trails, although I'm learning. I'm having trouble rooting myself in this landscape, probably because I sank my roots so deep into the landscape around my former home that it's going to take a while to recover.

But you don't make a place home without putting some effort into it. This isn't a landscape for mad infatuation; it's a landscape you learn to love. So I took myself out on Tuesday morning for a walk in the park.

The morning wasn't auspicious, overcast with a threat of rain, and the wind off the lake was strong and crisp. But it was still worth a try; besides, I have to learn this park before I can begin to love it, and the only way to do so is practice.

Overcast or not, I had it in mind to find joy there. In general, I figure if I look around the landscape with due attention joy is probably lurking somewhere: in the dodging and diving of swallows by the water's edge, in the marvelously complicated song of a red-breasted grosbeak (identified for me by a birder), in the accomplished soaring of gulls. I thought I'd skim the landscape, find a bit of joy, bring it home, and write it up, to round off a section of this book and (I hoped) balance out the darkness.

Of course, it didn't work that way. Does it ever? No matter how careful I was to deposit my personal baggage at the gate into the park, no matter how open I kept my eyes and ears and mind and heart, joy wasn't having any part of it. Not joy's problem; mine. I felt in the deep gut places of my soul the voice—the one that calls me "child"—whispering, *It's too soon. You aren't ready.*

OK, I can buy that. I'm no more ready for joy than someone a week out of major surgery is up for a nice long hike. There is such a thing as convalescence, and it takes time. I hadn't had anywhere near enough time yet.

Accepting where I was left me free to receive the gift, for of course there was a gift in the landscape; it just wasn't the gift I was looking for. (Which is par for the course.)

Milkweed. Specifically, milkweed in flower.

Now, milkweed—although it's invaluable, especially for monarch butterflies—is not an attractive plant at the best of times, and its flowers are not outstanding. They aren't the sort of blooms you'd break stride for. They're a sort of dull mauve, ball-shaped cluster atop the plant's broad, unimpressive leaves, no big deal.

But even though they are not present joy or beauty, they are a promise.

No, that's the wrong word. (That was the next gift.) Not a promise, a certainty.

Milkweed is never attractive, from seedling to gawky senescence, but it produces a yearly miracle: pods full of the most exquisite seeds, beautiful as the best brocade, lying close-lapped in the pod and topped by creamy, gleaming silk. Each fall, I look for pods of exactly the right ripeness, split them open in my hands, and spend a moment, lasting into eternity, re-entering into wonder.

I knew for absolutely certain that come the right day in October, a day when the sun is strong in a sky of the richest blue and we're still warm with the last touch of summer, I can come here and—again, for absolutely certain—find milkweed pods and their miraculous beauty.

Now, for me, this is major. I have had enough of promises. Promises are human; sometimes they work out and sometimes they don't. I had just come through a time of promises betrayed— more by mishap than by any bad intention, but that doesn't make it hurt any the less. I'd done some betraying of promises myself, which didn't help any. If anyone were to promise me that joy was on the way, I would probably smile politely and snort inwardly. *Yeah. Sure.*

But this certainty of milkweed goes beyond promises. This cannot be betrayed, because it's not of our making. It is on its own schedule. It doesn't rise in the human heart, and therefore it can't fail there.

Here was the joy in the landscape: an understanding, a grasp of something I don't think I'd ever properly grasped before. God does not make promises to us. Instead, God makes a covenant, and the covenant is not up for renegotiation or amendment. This goes far deeper than promises, right into the same certainty I had about the milkweed. I can count on God's love as I can count on the seasons cycling, the turn of the earth on its axis, the swing of the earth round the sun. Whatever befalls, God will be there: love to me, and in time that will be joy. It's just a matter of time.

I walked slowly back to the car, quiet in heart and listening to the birds, knowing I can wait, and mend, and learn to trust again.

CHAPTER 2

Being Human

I will sing of loyalty and of
justice;
to you, O Lord, I will sing.
I will study the way that is
blameless.
When shall I attain it?

—PSALM 101:1–2

❧ I Don't Wanna ❧

The leaves have come down in the narrow strip of wild yard next to the long side porch, a blanket of golden glory, glowing incandescent in the damp. I do not want to rake them.

Nor do I want to fix the broken towel bar in the downstairs bathroom. It's crudely attached to the wall by a pair of screws, and one of the screws has come out (as it always does) and gone missing. I do not want to go rooting around in the baskets of miscellaneous hardware in the storage closet, looking for the right kind of screw. I do not want to go through the toolbox looking for the right screwdriver.

I am not in the mood to put a new battery in the basement smoke detector. It's been squeaking for a couple of days now, a polite throat-clearing intermittent little "eep!" that sends the cats' ears rotating. I have the right sort of battery. It would take me half a minute to replace the old one. I don't want to do it. While I'm at it, I also don't want to clean out the refrigerator freezer, nor tidy the dining room sideboard, nor tackle the closets.

I do not want to get dinner. I've been getting dinner for years now; I used to enjoy it, but now it has begun to bore me. Similarly, I do not want to do the dishes, tidy the counters (a losing battle, anyway), mop down the stove top, sweep the kitchen floor. Even less do I want to think about rummaging through the cupboards, throwing out the old stuff, cleaning the shelves, and putting everything back in order. In fact, the very thought makes me want to go lie down.

I do not want even to *think* about getting the house ready for winter—getting the storm windows back from Jerry the painter, caulking windows, replacing weather stripping. I know that if this doesn't get done the house will be hideously drafty, but I don't care. I'll just put on extra socks, and if the other members of the family don't like it, *they* can caulk the windows.

I do not want to dust. I do not want to sort books. Ordinarily, I might not mind ironing some shirts, but not now. I especially, particularly do not wish to tidy, not even my own desk.

I am tired of being an adult. I am tired of responsibility, of forethought, of prudence, of making sure that what needs to get done gets done, or at least the bits I can't skip. I want to go back to being fifteen (although without the hormones, thank you). Alternatively, I'd like to go for a sea cruise—anything that takes me out of the house for a long, long time. Since neither of those is on, I'd at least like to go to bed for the afternoon with a book and a cup of hot mocha.

But I don't do that. There's a certain something in me that sighs and puts down the book and wanders off in search of the right-sized screw and a Robertson screwdriver. This same side of me automatically rinses and stacks dishes, puts something together for supper, checks on the kids' homework, and scoops an armload of laundry out of the dryer and sorts it. This is what adulthood is about: doing what you don't necessarily want to, because it needs to be done.

There is a similar part of me that won't let me cheat, lie, or be cruel to people without feeling lousy about it afterwards. There is a grammar of quite ordinary goodness that underlies the surface of much of society, thanks be to God, a default of decency. It may get forgotten at times, but it's still there. Not everyone follows it, and we all lapse sometimes, but when we do so most of us feel the rough wrongness in our moral syntax, a small stone in the sneaker, and it bothers us, sometimes only fleetingly but sometimes badly indeed. At least that's true of most of the people I know (although I can also think of a few really, *really* strange cases).

There is a part of me that is drawn irresistibly to love my children, and through them other children. This is pure instinct stuff. I can't claim any credit for it. I remember lying in my hospital bed with my new firstborn in my arms and feeling as though my neural wires were all being unplugged and re-routed through my hypothalamus. Through my own kids, other children become lovable. Through other children, still other and older children become lovable, and there is no one who is not an older child.

There is a part of me that gets drawn Godward no matter how whiny or doubtful I feel. St. Paul talks about the human condition: "I do not understand what I do; for I do not do what I want, but I do the very thing I hate" (Romans 7:15). That is, I know what God expects from me, but I seem to find myself charging off in the opposite direction without wanting to. But the opposite also applies: having once let God sneak into our lives, we find some changes. Although we may give ourselves permission to get down and play in the sandbox with the other snide little kids, it just doesn't feel right. Instead of doing the things we like and find easy, we may find ourselves pulled willy-nilly into doing the things that we're not so sure of, things that make us nervous, things that get us hurt or stretch us in a way that we don't find comfortable at all. But we do them because some inner sensor feels that *that* way lies God.

There is an instinctive itch, in all times and cultures, in all conditions of humankind: the still, small voice, the scent of the numinous, as haunting and fetching as the smell of leaves burning in autumn. This scent, this longing, this itch, this *something* grows stronger and stronger with time, habituating and yet more strongly satisfying, something for which the need becomes both stronger and more deliciously fulfilled. In this sense, I suppose religion really is the (endogenous) opiate of the people.

We spend much time trying to figure out where sin comes from—why we're all like Paul, not doing what we know is right, not doing what we want to do. But it doesn't occur to us to wonder why, in fact, we do as much good as we do. Our culture sometimes is fascinated by the dark and the macabre, to the point where we forget how mysterious the Light is—and so much more interesting! Not flat and glaring brightness, but a richness of colors defeating any prism. We are so fascinated by the problem of evil that we forget its equal and opposite problem, the problem of love. Where does it come from, love? Why are we drawn to be loving?

Once we have the scent of God, the smell of the living water, nothing else will quite do. Not that our pleasure in other things is diminished—quite the contrary. Delighting in God means delighting all the more deeply in God's creation, and in God's creation's creations, from the glory of grass snakes to the arc of the night sky. The pleasure we've been willing to put aside in the interests of finding that certain something—those pleasures we get back, all the happier.

In a properly God-directed mood—the sort of mood I get some mornings when the stars are properly configured and my meds are working perfectly—my strength is as the strength of ten and I can actually ream out whole closets. There's nothing like joy to make you busy and productive, and there's nothing like God for Joy.

☙ Hot and Cold ❧

Honestly, I can't complain. Thus far, it's been my kind of summer, cool with lots of rain. So when the thermometer ascended to reasonable, seasonable temperatures (middle eighties to you on Fahrenheit; top of the twenties for you Celsius types) for a couple of days there, I wasn't in any position to moan. At least not where anyone could hear me.

My friend Amanda was, however, delighted. The same weather that leaves me in a damp and miserable heap perks her right up. Her idea of heaven is sitting out on a Florida beach in a heat wave in mid-August, being fried. If she weren't so pretty, I'd be forced to ask myself if she weren't just possibly half-lizard. But because we are friends, I am happy for her when it heats up, and she takes some comfort, when it's cool and damp, that I am enjoying the weather.

It struck me that this is one of those rare human differences that nobody can read anything into. Nobody can judge a person as a wuss for not being able to handle the heat. Even we Canadians don't look down on someone made miserable by the cold; it's understandable, perfectly reasonable. Moral judgment or opinion doesn't enter into one's idea of comfy climatic conditions. It's not like diurnal rhythms; I'm always getting needled by the lark types for being a night owl ("Up at eight? The day's half over!"). I suspect that some night owls give lark types a hard time for being too goody two-shoes for words.

It seems to be normal human nature to define the group opposite to your own as somehow wanting or wrong. Most of us draw some of our sense of self-worth from fitting in with the prevailing decor; if the decor is turquoise, we are apt to find turquoise good. The problem is, we don't seem to be able to embrace the goodness of turquoise while also rejoicing in the goodness of (say) hot pink. Quite the contrary; we seem to need to define turquoise as good and hot pink as not-good, presumably because we're usually thinking in terms of a zero-sum game. That is, there's only so much goodness available, and if turquoise is to "win," then hot pink has to lose. From there, it becomes quite natural to find good reasons why hot pink is downright bad, to find moral and philosophical reasons to condemn hot pink, and to look for scientific evidence that hot pink is an aberration, or at least sub-par. We lapse into TEAPOT thinking—TEAPOT standing for "those evil, awful people over there." Then we drag God into it. Since we are turquoise and turquoise is good and hot pink is bad, therefore God must love and esteem turquoise and condemn hot pink (except maybe for a few special individuals of our liking).

But who we are—turquoise or hot pink, male or female, heavily pigmented or pale, gentile or Jew, short or tall, rich or poor, fat or skinny, gay or straight, Montague or Capulet—is not something we should have to answer for. It is profoundly unjust to hold a person accountable for something over which the person had no choice. What we *do* is another matter altogether, and for that we are accountable, and should be. What's astonishing is the strength of the human compulsion to judge others with neither mercy nor justice, simply because they are different from oneself.

There's a second and nastier variation on this theme. Let's say I decide that your hot pink is, by definition, inferior to my turquoise. So maybe I treat my hot-pink neighbors a little badly. Maybe I deny them some basic rights. Because I think hot pink is wrong, hot pink shouldn't have the vote. (Actually, what's really going on here is that I'm afraid hot pink dislikes me just as much as I dislike hot pink, so if the hot pinkers get the vote, my own turquoise interests may be threatened. But we won't talk about that.)

Nonetheless, I have to have some reason to give them (and myself) as to why hot pink shouldn't have the vote. Since not all hot pinkers have actually done anything to forfeit the vote, other than being hot pink, I have to prove to them that it's not what they've done; it's who they are that's the problem. The vote, I say, is not a right; it must be earned, and it's not something that hot pink *can* earn. This is because, as all civilized people know, hot pinkers are childlike, naïve, impulsive, uneducable, and prone to immorality and beastly excesses. The scientific proof: autopsies have shown that the hot pink brain is, on average, half a gram smaller than the turquoise brain, give or take a gram.

Or—much easier, because I don't have to find proof and can't be disproved—I can fall back on ontology: in God's great scheme of things, turquoise is clearly good and hot pink is bad, and here's a scripture verse to prove it. Eve was bad; therefore Eve's daughters are bad (one exception, Mary), and let's not notice that Eve had sons too; or maybe it's one of those sex-linked recessives. Therefore even when hot pink does exactly the same things that turquoise does, turquoise is still right and hot pink is still wrong, because hot pink is permanently stained by the ghostly, ineradicable flaw of hot pinkitude.

The worse I behave toward hot pinkers, the more I'm going to have to justify my behavior by blaming them for it. Why? Because the only alternative is to face the fact that I have been behaving like a real jerk for no good reason—or more likely, for self-serving reasons, which is something I do not want to admit to myself or anyone else. Especially to God. So I make God just as judgmental as I am, just as hateful of hot pink, because this way I'm off the hook. Permanently. This is why "hate the sin and love the sinner" simply doesn't work; we slide off sideways, like a car on glare ice, into loving the sin because it allows us all the self-indulgent fun of hating the sinner without having to feel bad about what we're doing. Very convenient.

But what I have forgotten in all this self-justification, this self-serving dishonesty, is that God created us all, hot pink and turquoise, and chrome yellow and magenta and mauve and every shade and variant of humankind. Yes, some of us are flawed and sick, but that's a state of the individual, not of a class. When we judge each other without even seeing each other as individual and precious humans—when we dismiss other human beings as inherently unworthy, without even bothering to get to know them as people—then we disrespect God's love for them. This is *really* disrespecting God, and if we're Christians at all, we know it's both wrong and deeply, deeply stupid.

I have got to learn to love my enemy. This means I have to sit down and accept that this person (who is not like me, with whom I disagree, who loves hot weather when cool weather is the only civilized climate) is also God's beloved child and is therefore fully worthy of my respect and attention—unless, of course, I claim to know better than God. Maybe this person is entitled to her spells of hot weather, even if they make me uncomfortable. Maybe this person has something to say that I should hear and ponder in my heart. Just possibly, this person may be more right than I am about one or two things.

It's messy, of course. In my middle age, I have decided that virtually everything that is spiritually right is messy, and that virtually everything that is extremely neat and orderly probably hasn't been kicked hard enough yet to show how messy it really is. Then again, I may just be trying to justify my own housekeeping.

Anyway. On my birthday, the temperature dropped back down to a civilized level and it promised to rain. Amanda is quite happy; she's had a taste of real summer heat, and there's still all of August to come.

❧ Mixed Signals ❧

I remember back when I was home-schooling a child, I would take him now and again to the Museum of Science and Technology in the city. We'd both enjoy ourselves fooling around with the exhibits (which are delightfully hands-on). One afternoon, as he played electronic hockey, I found myself fiddling with one of the hands-on radio exhibits. This particular exhibit showed how sound waves interact. By turning this dial or that, you could get waves to reinforce each other (producing a pure tone) or overlap in a peculiar way (giving a mixed tone). Or you could, by positioning the waves just so, get them to cancel each other out completely.

Fascinating. My mind is always ready to leap for a metaphor, like a frog's tongue for a fly on the wing (that's a simile, but you see my point). Here was an absolutely splendid one for something that drives me crazy.

In real life, the signals we get from (and give) each other are often mixed in such a way as to self-cancel. "I'm being honest with you" is a line that automatically makes me suspicious. We damn with faint praise; we learn to sugarcoat our salt; we slip the little dig into the middle of apparent bonhomie, camouflaging it with jokiness so that the recipient won't notice when the blade slips betwixt the ribs. Then there's always the immortal one: "I love you, dear, in spite of all your failings and faults and personal problems, in spite of the burden you are to me." Oh, that's a real sweetie, that one.

The technical term for this is "cognitive dissonance," and it is deeply crazy making. It's confusing; it pulls you both ways until you're not sure which way is north or whether the sun rises in the west. To change similes, it's like having two completely different pieces of music playing in your head at the same time. We've probably all had to live with this at some time or another. We've probably all done it to others too.

What are the reasons for mixed signals? Fear comes to mind first: we're afraid that if we're truthful we'll be cruisin' for a bruisin'—and indeed, this fear does come true sometimes. Or it's the social conventions we've been brought up to regard as law: "Don't air your dirty linen"; "If you can't say something nice, don't say anything at all." Good manners do indeed grease the skids of existence, but they can also confuse the issue. They are, after all, intended to preserve our social masks, not to reveal the truth.

Or the problem may be our own confusion. Our feelings about another person may be terribly ambivalent: loving and hating, needing and fearing. We may cling desperately to causes and people while hating them for our dependency on them—a state that can drive the recipient around the bend. Or we may not know how we feel at all. Sometimes I think I'm fronting the world with a calm and pleasant face, while everyone around me can tell that

I'm really upset and angry. When I don't want to deal with my personal dragons and instead insist on turning my back on them, they have a habit of peeking over my shoulder and frightening innocent bystanders—and then I can't figure out why people get upset (duh!).

Or finally—least frequently, I hope—the problem may be simple evil. People may use mixed signals to manipulate and control others, undercut them (and often thus keep them obediently captive), and get their own way. Using crazy-making tactics is a notable feature of most forms of abuse. It's no accident that Satan is called the Father of Lies.

It may be some comfort to realize that poor old St. Paul had to struggle with similar issues. It seems that church politics—which can, as we all know, be quite stunningly nasty—go back to the beginning. Paul faced a mess in the church in Corinth: his authority was being undermined and his motives called into question (2 Corinthians 1:15–2:2). He is hurt; he writes with "many tears," and he postpones his planned visit rather than risk another confrontation.

He has been accused, he says, of saying yes and no—of giving mixed messages. But, says Paul, I don't do this. I don't do this because God doesn't say "yes, yes" and "no, no"; I don't say one thing out of one side of my mouth and another out of the other, and neither does God. He gave us the Word, and the Word was a great big unequivocal *yes*. God's message was Christ Jesus, and Jesus is a yes without a trace of no anywhere, because God knows his own, and it is us.

We may see God as confusing, or two-sided, or even hypocritical—judging and loving, angry and tender, distant and intrusive, omnipotent and helpless to keep us from harm, withholding forgiveness and demanding that we forgive. God can look terribly two-faced at times. But this isn't God's problem; it's our perception, which is clouded by our own confusion or need to keep love for ourselves and see our enemies pounded into applesauce. We load our own issues, baggage, and confusion onto God and then complain that *God's* got a problem. Oh. Right.

God's message isn't "I love you, but . . ." or "I'd love you if . . ." or "I'll love you when. . . ." It's simply "I love you." It is love without illusions; it goes right past the masks that we want others to stop at, on into our core, whether or not we want the Light shining there. We can accept it or reject it, but we can't make it conditional for ourselves or anyone else. It is love so intimately entwined with knowledge and truthfulness that we can't part the strands. Christ Jesus and the Holy Spirit speak to us straight, clearly, and truthfully. Therefore we can trust and relax our need to control, however unclear or confusing life seems to be.

But there isn't the slightest shade of no in God's unending yes. Paul is very sure of that. We are God's, created and redeemed by love. The only reasonable thing we can say in response is a great big unequivocal *yes*.

🌿 The Teapot 🌿

Some time ago I treated myself to a tea set in blue-and-white Chinese porcelain. You've seen the stuff if you've ever gone into a Chinese grocery store. Before firing, each piece has had grains of rice pressed right into the wet clay, forming geometrical patterns of soft opacity. The china itself is commonplace and inexpensive, but it's very pretty and has a classical, restful, even serene, feeling about it. My teapot and its matching cup and saucer are a little more dressed up, with small sunbursts of the thinnest scarlet lines and bands of what looks like metallic gold.

Now I warmed the pot, set out the cup and saucer, and put water on to boil for tea. I thought, as I waited, how mixed my feelings are about things like my teapot. On the one hand, I subscribe morally and intellectually to the notion that less is best. Things aren't meant to be small gods and Martha Stewart is an extremely (shall we say) misguided spiritual guru. Our Lord told us to hit the road taking not even a walking stick or a spare pair of sandals. But that's not how we operate. It wasn't until I had to go through a houseful of stuff, sorting and getting rid of things and packing the remainder for the movers, that I realized how much stuff there was. Stuff seems to breed more stuff, just as single socks apparently migrate via the power grid from one clothes dryer to another, reappearing transmogrified into clothes hangers in the backs of closets, where they then self-replicate like rabbits.

More seriously, I understand how our consumer culture creates massive environmental problems, simultaneously feeding on and driving the inequities in wealth that warp the spirits of both those who have too much and those who have too little. I know too that the sort of transient, greedy self-soothing that a person can grab by going shopping isn't really much different from the problematic self-soothing a person grabs in reaching for a bottle of scotch or a box of chocolates—God knows, I'm as susceptible to such temptation as anyone else.

It's not that stuff is bad in and of itself; it's what it makes us get up to that's the problem. It's like sex or nuclear power: it isn't the thing itself, it's what we do with it, what our choices make of us, and how it all affects the rest of the world around us. Stuff isn't the problem. It's our feelings about stuff that get us into trouble.

This teapot is hardly up to Martha's high standards; it's a cheap little piece of mass-produced pottery. Or is it? The pot itself is silent; it can't tell me whether the rice grains were pressed into the clay by a machine or by someone's fingers. It can't say how the blue geometrical bands got applied to it, or the scarlet sunbursts or the lines of gold. I have no idea where it was made, or by whom. In a sense, this ordinary teapot is an object of mystery.

What I do know is that using this teapot always propels me into a sort of mindfulness, forcing me to stop in my tracks and think about things I don't always give enough attention to: the poverty of third-world workers and their often horrible working conditions, for instance. Have I fed the pattern by buying this ware, or have I merely contributed my money to an economy that needs it? When I pour tea from this pot, I am acutely aware of the hands that made it, decorated it, glazed it, fired it, set it to cool, packed it. Were these people happy, or miserable, or just doing their job with their mind on more important things? I hope they take some satisfaction in producing this stuff. But again, I don't know.

I am aware of the environmental devastation common in countries where people are too caught up in bare survival to think about what they're doing to this earth. I am aware of the inequities from which I benefit, sometimes at bitter cost to others: of the astonishing, undeserved good fortune of being born white, middle-class, and North American into a family that valued its daughters and saw to their education. I may whinge about my own hardships, but they pale into nothing compared to the hardships faced by people like those who made my teapot.

I am acutely aware too of the strangeness and splendor of a country and culture so far removed from mine, so much older and (in many ways) wiser, a country that has suffered at a depth and intensity I cannot begin to imagine. Even at the trickle-down bottom of mass production, this china really is beautiful—to my eyes, more beautiful in its poverty, delicacy, and humility than the finest Worcester, which says much about the culture that produced it. It's good to be mindful of this too.

Holding my warm teapot and looking at it with love, I am also aware of the shadow side of asceticism: of how self-denial can transmute into the sin of pride, of how righteous indignation can be just good old nasty self-righteousness. Certainly there can be an antimaterialism that's simply destructive joylessness, the sort of raging Puritanism that blows up statues of the Buddha and bashes out stained-glass windows. It's really pride and anger with a big unacknowledged pinch of envy. Not spiritually healthy at all. I should know; I've been there.

Maybe what my teapot is supposed to do in my life is cultivate this sort of mindfulness, to remind me to be painfully, lovingly aware of this world's real suffering beauty and of my own prejudices and blinkered vision. Its humility should keep me humble; its beauty should remind me of delight.

The teapot came with a matching cup and saucer, a hybrid between formal European ware and Chinese blue-and-white, and like most mongrels they are incongruous and totally charming. It is sometimes a tiny but great pleasure to drink Lapsang Souchong from a teacup with a saucer, not from a pragmatic mug. Not always, just sometimes. I pour myself out a cup and sit back to plan the rest of my day.

⚘ The Bar ⚘

Now that renovations to the main part of the house are more or less done, we've been slowly clearing out the former rec room downstairs, where our boxes lived while we were a work in progress. Gradually we've uncovered the room's main feature: a large, glass-topped, paneled bar, clearly some former owner's pride and joy. It's hideous, and it takes up a great deal of space. So I invited the nice guys from Habitat for Humanity to pop around to take a look at the thing, with a view toward recycling it. On Thursday a middle-aged guy named Larry showed up to judge how useful the bar's materials could be and how easily they could be removed. He noticed immediately, as I had not, that it had a built-in electrical outlet.

Oh.

Trouble. Damn.

I don't "do" electricity. Oh, I use it plenty; who doesn't? I know some practical bits and pieces, like the fact that an adapter has to have the correct voltage for the thing you're plugging into it. I know that a circuit has to be complete or it won't work. I can change light bulbs and fuses and flip a circuit breaker. But at a fundamental level, probably like most people, I find electricity mysterious and more than a little frightening. I wouldn't dream of trying to replace a light fixture; I'd be too frightened that electricity would come streaming out, enraged by my presumption, and burn the house down.

Larry, on the other hand, is clearly quite comfortable with the stuff. Using a small fan and flipping circuit breakers, he determined that the bar's outlet was the only one on a later addition to the circuit box and could easily be isolated and dealt with. No problem.

As I watched him, I remembered the kid who did most of the wiring during the upstairs renovations, a young man (no older than my elder son) who has done his coursework and apprenticeship and is about to get his trade certification. He knew exactly what he was doing, and he did it quickly and well. After he finished installing a light fixture, the electricity would stay properly channeled and controlled in it, doing its right work of power, heat, and illumination.

Lightning strikes aside, the problem (when there is one) with electricity isn't with the stuff itself; it's just fine the way it is. No, the problem is what we do with it—our failure to handle it right, to give it enough thought and knowledge and care, to invest in sound copper wiring, well insulated. Or we may even assume that we don't need to give it thought, knowledge, care or investment; we may believe that we can toss the stuff around however we please without ill consequences. Or we may assume that we know enough, when we don't. That's when we set ourselves up for trouble.

Why does this remind me so much of love?

Look around and you can see humans doing each other damage, frequently out of hatred, greed, self-righteousness, indifference, but also out of love. Intimate enemies: parents and children, siblings, friends, mates, all supposedly loving each other but all screwing each other up, sometimes abominably. Watch parents and young children in Wal-Mart or on the bus; sometimes you'll see some parents doing the work of love and doing it well, but often you'll see the opposite. It gets terribly depressing sometimes. In line at the supermarket the other day, I watched a bored young mother and her three-year-old daughter. The child was trying to get Mum's attention, growing first restive and then increasingly upset when Mum completely ignored her, working herself up for the sort of tantrum that would prompt a maternal blast. I wanted to shake the mother and say, "Don't you see what message you're giving the kid—that she doesn't matter?"

The problem is that we've set up love as a matter of feeling, not of doing; as long as we feel loving, it's easy to behave lovingly. But sometimes we have to be loving when we don't feel like it— when we're tired, fed up, out of being in love, or totally centered on our own egotistical need to be served and to control. Then it's too easy to get sloppy, become inattentive, and act or speak without thinking, even while we tell ourselves that we're being good and loving. It's like doing a sloppy job of wiring in a fixture.

Everyone has off moments; the question is which predominates. God knows, the conversation of small children is not stimulating; mates have a way of being irritating, even enraging; and friendship requires the same sort of tending that a garden does.

Every one of us has a problem with selfishness; the only questions are how big the problem is, how honest we are about it, and how much we're willing to work against it. Sometimes we don't think it's a problem at all, and that's not great. But sometimes we try to hide our selfishness behind the pretense of love—pretending to ourselves, to God, and to others—and that is really deadly.

I used to think of electricity as behaving a little like water, which is one way of looking at it; but it misses an important difference. A small leak in the plumbing is a problem, but a small leak in the wiring is dangerous. Maybe honest indifference is less dangerous than love mishandled; I don't know. I do know that love mishandled can cause tremendous pain.

I also know that all love is inherently good; it all begins in God. Our job is to become the best conduit we can be for it, reducing our resistance and increasing our capacity. Love itself is never a problem; it's our pretense to be loving when in fact we aren't, or our ignorance of love's practical implications, that does the damage.

I know too that on the whole we are getting better at understanding what love should look like and managing it better. We (well, many of us) no longer believe that the loving thing to do to small babies is to leave them crying in their cribs. We don't believe in "spare the rod and spoil the child" anymore, nor in the rightness of racial segregation, nor in the right of a husband to beat his wife—just as we no longer believe that aluminum wiring is just as good as copper. We've learned a thing or two, although we still have a long, long way to go.

As always, the person I should be addressing this to is me.

Larry thinks he can come back with some help and a truck next week and get rid of the bar. I'll get the electrician in to deal with the outlet and its circuit; I don't "do" electricity. I know how little I know, and that's the way it should be.

❧ The Baby ❧

Waah. Waah. Waah.

The baby's crying caught my ear the moment I walked into the grocery store. What struck me immediately was how steady the crying was, how regular—and how utterly uninflected. It was a buzz-saw sort of crying, not screaming with rage or wailing in pain or anything of that sort. Just a steady waah, waah, waah.

Ah—there they were, in the vegetable section: mother, father, infant in carrier perched in the fold-up section of the grocery cart. Mother was a strikingly almost-pretty young woman in her early or mid twenties; father was a tough-looking guy a fair bit older. They were having an animated discussion over the onions while their infant howled on, unheeded.

It bothered me a lot—not that the baby was crying; babies *do* cry, after all. But it seemed very much as though all concerned were so used to this situation that they all took it for granted, the baby included. The father, who was wheeling the cart, bounced the carrier occasionally, but otherwise neither parent paid the least attention to the child. I thought I heard in the baby's cry a certain resignation ("I'll go on howling because I do need to be cared for, but I don't expect them to do anything about it").

I shouldn't have been surprised or upset, and I had to rein in my own easy middle-class tendency to turn judgmental. This is Food Basics, a decent, cheap supermarket serving the part of the city with funky housing, drug issues, and a population with serious problems—the walking wounded, parolees and their families, the unhospitalized mentally ill, the poor. This neighborhood is not Functional Family City. Going by clothing, I'd say this young family was in poverty.

Now, I don't for a moment think that poverty in and of itself makes a person an inadequate parent; I've seen equally negligent parenting in prosperous suburban shops, after all. I remember seeing the same pattern once in an Indian restaurant over near the university; in that case, dress and location suggested that the parents were most likely either young faculty or older graduate students. It wasn't an inexpensive restaurant, and they were well dressed. But they were just as self-absorbed and just as unresponsive to their three kids, who were running wild, unchecked, a two-year-old disappearing off somewhere, unheeded, into the restaurant's rear quarters and being brought back by one of the waiters; his older sister bursting into tears at the table, and her father literally turning away from her, stony-faced, uninterested. The incident haunted me for weeks. I don't know what the family's history was like. I can make some fair guesses about its future.

Poverty does strain families, mostly by putting parents (especially single parents, who are usually women) under intense stress. It's much harder to be a steady, structured, nurturing parent when you're scrambling to find affordable housing and at your wits' end by the week before the welfare check arrives.

But still it bothered me, how neither parent responded to the child—how all three of them were apparently taking the crying so much for granted. It bothered me for the same reason that it bothers me when I see this behavior anywhere: What on earth are the parents saying to the child here? "You don't matter." "We're not interested." Inevitably, the child takes on all the blame for the problem. It doesn't matter if this is not what they intend to say; it's what the child inevitably hears, usually with discouraging consequences for the child's emotional well-being.

How, in God's name, are children supposed to learn that they're valuable in their own and God's eyes if they aren't valuable to their parents? How can they learn to see themselves as precious and particular when those who are supposed to love them can't be bothered to pick them up and comfort them when they're distressed? How can they develop any healthy sense of self-worth?

Why on earth do we get our knickers so hopelessly knotted about sex and doctrinal orthodoxy and all that stuff when there is so much of this sort of sadness in the world—so many children going untended, so many infants wailing steadily with no expectation that loving arms will stretch down to comfort them? Compared to our catastrophic failure to love and take care of these little ones, our arguments over doctrinal purity look to me like a colossal waste of time and energy. One-fifth of the children in my Canadian province live in poverty. Like the parents in the supermarket, we tune out the crying; like the parents in the Indian restaurant, we turn our backs on their distress. God must weep a whole lot.

The infant's crying went on steadily, without change in timing, intensity, or tone as I went up and down aisles, getting together my cartload of dinner materials. The young family fetched up at the next cash register just as I did. The baby was still crying exactly as it was when I entered the store, the same steady, uninflected, punctuated waah-waah-waah. I paid for my groceries and then remembered that I'd meant to get the Saturday paper, so I had to pay for it separately.

"Sorry about that," I told the middle-aged cashier. "I wasn't concentrating."

"I know," she said back, with a dark, direct look. "It's the crying."

❧ Yum ❧

I promise myself each year not to start thinking about Christmas until at least the third week in Advent, but it's difficult when you're in choir. This year, we're doing a John Rutter piece for Christmas Eve, and we need to get going on it.

I don't like everything John Rutter writes; some of it strikes me as being banal or hokey or too chipper, like animated elevator music. But the man does have a gift for one particular style of choral work: a style that conveys stillness, sweetness, and deep longing. The piece we're doing for Christmas Eve is like that. It's easy music, too—in general, Rutter isn't what I'd call challenging. It's what I've heard called "grateful" music; it makes a choir sound better than it really is. (Ungrateful music, on the other hand, is music that takes real work and still doesn't sound particularly good.)

You hear a fair bit of Rutter around Christmas, especially his carol "What Sweeter Music," which is one of his best and best-known pieces, and a very lovely one indeed. It makes a nice change from the *Messiah*. But it does more than that. Music like this is appealing, I think, because it calls out to something most of us have: a longing for things to be *good*.

Yes, as M. Scott Peck says, "life is difficult," but that's not what we want. Of course we want things to be calm and stress-free and unproblematic. But it's more than that. We want our world to be harmonious and peaceful, lions cuddling up with lambs, love diffused throughout the landscape, as richly sweet and satisfying as Rutter's music at its best.

I don't think it's just a shallow, childish Santa-level wish; I think it's a really deep desire, a holy longing. We sense that there is a rightness of things, and that this world isn't there yet, and the music whispers to us that it's possible. We long for it: the Peaceable Kingdom.

There's a problem with this longing, though. I think we tend to focus on the Virgin and the Christ Child, the angels and shepherds, the whisper of "peace on earth, good will to men" as something isolated, set apart—in two senses.

First, we set it apart from the rest of the story. Richard Wilbur's poem got it right: this child will be glorified and abandoned, will be tortured and crucified, and will break the bonds of death. It's all one piece, and you can't take one part of it and forget about the rest. This "gentle Mary meek and mild" (I doubt if she really was, but that's another piece) will have swords driven through her heart and will stand helplessly by to receive her child's whipped and bloody body. The whole story is anything but sweet and peaceful. But in our longing for the Peaceable Kingdom, we shut out thinking about the cost.

Second, we allow ourselves to long for the Peaceable Kingdom only for a week or two at Christmas, and we tend to turn the longing into sentimentality, not into a passionate desire to make this Kingdom *happen* on an immediate and practical level. It becomes an aesthetic and emotional matter, the spiritual equivalent of a glass of Bailey's Irish Cream, not a rubber-to-the-road affair of tumbling the haughty from their seats and exalting the humble and meek. God forbid we should actually *do* something about this longing; it would set the world all topsy-turvy, and besides, what would it do to our taxes?

The Peaceable Kingdom is not going to happen in this world without our active participation, which means first and foremost our refusal to accept that "business as usual" is the right way of doing things. It means working passionately against injustice, violence, and oppression; it means standing with the poor instead of sitting in judgment of them. The Peaceable Kingdom, as Christ pointed out repeatedly, is not going to be easily or peacefully achieved; it's going to require pain, unsettledness, and discordance, the opposite of Rutter's sweet harmonies, because it lies in opposition to what we really deeply treasure: our own comfort, our own selfishness. We can't have our treasure and satisfy the longing. We have to choose.

We do choose, year after year: we choose the treasure, not the Kingdom. In less than a month, we'll be back to business as usual, the longing for the Kingdom put away with *Messiah* and *Charlie Brown's Christmas* and the Rutter CDs and the creche set.

With any luck, though, the longing for the Kingdom may have changed someone in some way that will make the person work toward the Kingdom. Enough small changes, and who knows what might happen?

I know one thing for certain: I'll enjoy the Rutter we're singing, and I'll sing it well—as I said, it's not difficult. I'll listen to other bits of Rutter, and I may even buy a small bottle of Bailey's to sip as I listen. But after dark on Christmas Eve, I will pull out my *real* Christmas music. It's a dark, difficult, demanding piece, a piece full of the sweet wildness of hedge roses and of discords as sharp as a crown of thorns; it brims with the mystery of poverty and grace. I haven't sung it out loud since I was a girl (my voice is too deep for it now) but I can summon it to my mind's ear whenever I wish, because it lives there. The music is Benjamin Britten's; the words are Robert Southwell's. This is the twentieth century married to the sixteenth.

> *Behold, a silly tender babe*
> *In freezing winter night,*
> *In homely manger trembling lies:*
> *Alas, a piteous sight.*
> *With joy approach, O Christian wight,*
> *Do homage to your King,*
> *And highly praise this humble pomp*
> *Which he from heaven doth bring.*

❧ Psalm 175(a) ❧

(A psalm by Molly Wolf upon the Psalms of David)
I said unto my soul, "Come thou my soul, and let us look;
let us look unto the psalms of David,
of David, King of Israel.

For in the psalms there are said many things
upon which a writer might profitably ponder.
Consider, my soul, and take upon thee
the beauty and the power of the psalms of David,
For in them thou wilt find inspiration,
the seed of which thou mayest plant
And raise up to thyself more essays,
essays to make glad the heart of thine Editor,
To make Marketing sing with joy and play upon the cistern
and dance in the hallways and elevators of thy Publisher."
And so I went unto the psalms of David
and looked upon them most straitly and with care.
And lo! No inspiration did I find within them,
no seed from which to raise up fruitful essays;
Nay, only vexation did I find therein,
vexation and trouble for my soul.
For they were full of vindictiveness,
of cries for the punishment of David's enemies,
of enmity and the desire for revenge.
Full were they too of special pleading
and of the making of desperate bargains with the Lord God.
"Oh God, my Lord, if I am very good
and sacrifice and make prayers to thee
and repent me of my sins,
O Lord my God, wilt thou then extract me from this
trouble?
Wilt thou prithee lay waste to the lands of those that
hate me?
Wilt thou, for my sake, ensure that the Bad Guys get theirs?

I pray thee, Lord, that their camels starve,

that scabies afflict their sheep, and PMS the flesh of their
    women.

I pray thee, Lord, that their offspring shrivel like slugs upon
    rock salt,

like slugs upon the salt desert of the Negev."

This is what I read among the psalms of David

and was sore troubled in mine inmost parts,

So that all the songs of David seemed corrupted,

not one of them free from the shadow of desire

from the desires of selfishness and anger.

They spoke to me with power and truth of where I mayst
    now be,

but it is not the place I most desire to be.

The psalms are raw;

the psalms describe the state of the human heart.

The psalms betray our heart's blackest desires;

the psalms are full of vengefulness and magical thinking.

The psalms speak beauty,

when they speak of the dust of thy being,

of thy dependence upon the Lord thy God.

The psalms sing truly

when they speak of the greatness and majesty of the Lord,

of the Lord made manifest in Her Creation.

The psalms are true and maddening,

full of honesty, however disastrous.

The psalms speak of the truths of the human heart,

of thy heart that requireth by times of the Lord thy God

a swift corrective smack upside thy head.

I heard in my heart
the Lord speaking thus to David
"Wise up, O my child! Thine enemy too is my child,
he who hateth thee is also my beloved.
His offspring too, and the woman of his tent,
his manservant and maidservant,
even his camels and sheep.
These too are my creatures,
they too pray to me
in the heat of the day, in the soul's desperation.
They pray to be freed from thine oppression,
from thine enmity and persecution,
from the plagues that thou hast laid upon them.
As for delivering thee from thine affliction,
Remember thou, my child, how thou fetched up
in thy current predicament.
For they please Me who take responsibility
for the messes that they make.
Consider well, O David, if thou hast made the bed
in which thou now liest."
And David said to the Lord
"I will turn to my God in more humility, saying,
'O Lord my God, I had forgotten
that I am not the navel of the universe.
May it be to me according to thy will.
May I remember that I am only one among many.
May I remember how I have provoked mine enemy,
and look to him for forgiveness
and make peace.'"

And the Lord said to David,
Knowing full well the human heart
"So sayeth thou now, beloved.
Talk we again next Tuesday."
(here endeth the psalm)

CHAPTER 3

⁂

Truths and Illusions

*I know, O Lord, that your
judgments are right,
and that in faithfulness you
have humbled me.
Let your steadfast love become
my comfort
according to your promise
to your servant.*

—PSALM 119:75–76

❧ Belief ❧

Chrissie called just as I was starting to get supper ready. "Is it all right if I talk?" she asked anxiously. "Sure," I said, wedging the portable phone between ear and shoulder and getting on with the potatoes.

Chrissie and I have some things in common. We both broke out of very bad marriages. We've both spent time as single parents living with a lot of financial insecurity. We're also active, believing Christians. But there the resemblance has, in the past, ended. My church has a strong tradition of thoughtfulness, moderation, and tolerance. I like being an Anglican; I like the fact that our corner of the Kingdom expects that your mind goes to church along with the rest of you—that God expects you to use the loaf God gave you. I like the fact that we stay uncomfortably on the fence, refusing to turn our backs on members of the church who are not like us, refusing to stick only to the green pastures of easy camaraderie while there's the hard, painful work of inclusion to be done. I like having a set of core beliefs I hold onto with all my heart and mind and strength: that God is love, that Jesus Christ is God incarnate, that the Holy Spirit moves within us, that Scripture is full of the deepest sort of truth. I have a very strong sacramental streak, which Anglicanism satisfies. I like mystery and paradox, and the fact that Anglicanism doesn't insist on explaining and specifying *everything*. Then, of course, there's the music.

Chrissie comes from a conservative charismatic Christian background, one that sets high value on manifestations of the Spirit—speaking in tongues, being "slain in the Spirit," really exciting stuff that makes my solid Anglicanism look a bit dull and bland. Her tradition preaches that the Bible is word-for-word literally true, that the way is hard and narrow, and that transgressors will burn in Hell forever and ever. It sets a high value on wifely obedience and strictness in child rearing. It warns constantly about temptation and self-indulgence. It does not allow questioning, which (it believes) is Satan at work—and Satan is very much alive and with us.

But Chrissie's faith and Chrissie's gut are on bad terms these days, and church is a place that leaves her feeling confused and empty. Chrissie knows what her marriage was like; she *knows* how bad it was. Her church hands her only condemnation for "breaking her marriage vow," not the support and comfort she knows she needs; her pastor chides her for "wanting her freedom" and for forgetting that "whom God has joined together, let no man put asunder." Her church's "divorce support" program strenuously pushes for reconciliation as the only really acceptable outcome. Chrissie has been told that divorce is unforgivably sinful except (maybe) in cases of adultery or extreme abuse, though even then forgiveness is more Christian. Her mother tells her that "God hates divorce."

Chrissie's gut, on the other hand, tells her that God does not want people to live the way she lived with her neglectful dry-drunk husband; this is not what marriage is meant to be. Chrissie's gut tells her that God is in favor of life, not death; God understands and forgives her and knows that she did her absolute best to make the marriage work. Nor can she read her Bible and take everything in it as literal truth. Some stuff feels absolutely true. Some stuff makes a fair bit of sense, but it doesn't feel like hard data. Some stuff feels very much like ordinary human beings being quite ordinarily human. She cannot, for example, imagine a God who wants to bash a baby's head out on a rock, but there it is, in black and white.

The quarrel between gut and church is terribly wearing for her. She feels guilty all the time; she must be wrong to question, to doubt, to have thoughts that clash so badly with her beliefs. It's as though she doesn't fit in anymore.

What she wants to hear from me, now and again, is that this sort of doubt is OK. You are not going to Hell, Chrissie, for wanting to be loved. God is not waiting to zap you if you notice that there are places where the Bible isn't perfectly internally consistent. It is OK to struggle and have doubts, because it's in struggling and doubting that we often find how true Scripture can be, but in a deeper, wiser, richer sense than literal fact-type truth could ever be. It is OK to trust your head and your gut instincts, and no, this is not Satan at work in you. It is OK *not* to feel perfectly happy and obedient, not to whitewash trouble so it tries to look like joy; look at the Book of Job!

What my corner of Christianity gives me, and her corner of Christianity has denied Chrissie, is what God gave us all: free will. I can, without being heaved out of church, question certain traditional beliefs; or I can decide to accept them without questioning because I'm willing to trust my forebears in faith—but I don't have to buy the whole enchilada. I can (and do) accept the Virgin Birth and the Resurrection; I certainly accept them in the deepest, most central way, the way of great poetry. If they were proved to be factually false, it wouldn't greatly bother me one way or another; the deep truth that they represent would remain. I can, on the other hand, question traditional views on sexuality, believing that as our understanding develops, some of our beliefs may change. I have that freedom, thanks be to God.

Chrissie's church is more controlling, and much more fearful. So it insists that it's the whole enchilada or no enchilada at all. This is why Chrissie's gut and her faith are locked in an exhausting, debilitating struggle with each other. For Chrissie is being faced with *choice,* and choice is what her church wants most strenuously to avoid.

I have come to believe that belief is a matter of choice. I know that seems strange at first, but think about it. We have two propositions, equally incapable of absolute proof: that there is a God (Option A), or that there is no God (Option B).

Nobody says that you *must* choose Option A, the God option. If God wanted to force us all into Option A, God wouldn't have given us free will. It's extremely easy to see that taking away any choice is control, and control is not love. I cannot believe in a God who would, even for our own good, coerce us into belief. I can believe in a God who completely wants us to choose God, who is ultimately so attractive that we'd be utterly nuts *not* to choose God, but who leaves the choosing up to us.

Nor can I believe in a God who would choose to condemn us for unbelief or mistaken belief. Too many good souls have never heard the Gospel proclaimed at all; too many have heard a "gospel" proclaimed that Jesus would have repudiated with anger. For too many, Christianity was a force for social conformity, European colonialism, exploitation, oppression. I can't quarrel with those who, for this reason, have chosen Option B. If anyone needs to take the blame for the choice, I think it's we Christians.

Having made the first choice, we then face a whole series of choices: do I stay over here with the agnostics, or do I join a particular spiritual tradition? Again, I can't believe in a God who loves us so little that we'd go to hell for making a reasonable-but-wrong choice. But I choose to believe that some ways of being spiritual are more rewarding or productive than others, and that a person generally does better in community than out of it.

Moreover, I believe that my Islamic and Buddhist and Aboriginal and Jewish and other faith-tradition brethren and sistren may have a fair bit of insight into this God business, and though we may disagree on the details we are still looking at the same reality, the same light. Islam sees it as a pure white light; I, as a Christian, see it as passed through the prism of the Incarnation and in radiant color. But it's still the same light.

So: I have chosen to believe in God. I have chosen to stay with the faith of my origins, Christianity, because it makes sense to me, and I have chosen to stay in the denomination in which I was raised because it's a really good place to play with theology. But I respect choices different from my own. I do this because ultimately I believe in a God of love who delights in every human soul and who has the capacity to forgive honest error—which God had better do, in fact, because none of us has this entirely right.

This is where Chrissie's church and I *really* part company. We all have some grasp of the truth of God, but absolutely none of us has God completely taped. This too is all right, because a God who we've got completely figured out is a God who is smaller than we are, when in fact God is immeasurably bigger than we are—and God, knowing that, knows how we struggle to get our minds around Godself, always wanting, never succeeding.

We struggle with things that don't make sense to us, as Chrissie is struggling now; this isn't apostasy (denying God) but theology (exploring God). It's an intensely personal business and, to my mind, about as much fun as a person can have with her clothes on. When Chrissie wrestles with her beliefs, she is wrestling as Jacob wrestled on the riverbank; she is *engaging* with God, on a real and personal level, with head and heart and everything she's got.

This, it seems to me, is what her church has trouble with. That church's God is one whose love is totally conditional; if we don't get it exactly right, then God will punish us. It's a theology of fear, based on a vindictive deity who demands perfection and will settle for nothing less. It's a zealous faith, and I have to credit its energy and passionate desire for the right. But it's missed something fundamental, I believe: that the Abba proclaimed by Jesus is a God of mercy and forgiveness, who cares far more that we've got our priorities right than about whether we got 98 percent on the final.

Mind you, this is not to say that all belief systems are equally good; you would have to be either blind or deluded to live in this world and accept that. Just think Osama bin Laden or David Koresh. There is an enormous amount of really terrible theology around, and it has dreadful outcomes. "By their fruits you shall know them" works for me. The faiths that I respect have in common the central qualities of justice and mercy, compassion and humility, deep devotion to human realities, and (above all) faith that our Creator loves us deeply and forever. This is what I've chosen to believe, and I'm happy with my choices.

Chrissie will find her way. Once a soul starts on the journey she's embarked on, the journey itself is apt to become so fascinating and rewarding that the soul gets drawn deeper and deeper into the process. She's moving Godward in the pilgrim way, increasingly dauntless and full of joy.

My True Love Hath My Heart

It's a lovely poem by Sir Philip Sidney, who lived and died four hundred and some years ago. The first verse (slightly modernized) goes:

> My true love hath my heart, and I have his,
> By just exchange, one for the other given,
> I hold his dear, and mine he would not miss;
> There never was a better bargain driven.

You could rephrase this in terms more suited to contemporary social sciences ("my significant other and I have arrived at a mutual understanding of our emotional investment in each other"), but that's missing on a few cylinders, not just in terms of beauty but also in terms of meaning. Sidney is saying something about deep and serious attachment, but he says it poetically, not literally, and therefore with greater depth and truthfulness.

We lost something, back in the early modern era—somewhere in the 1800s, at a guess, but don't hold me to that. What we lost is an understanding of what poetic truth is about. We used to have no problems with metaphor or simile; they were, in fact, considered higher and more valuable forms of truth, because they have such beauty and power. Just look at Shakespeare. When he wants to say something with a lot of depth, he reaches for a really ripe metaphor.

But something went wrong when we elevated mere facts to the highest position, facts we could prove scientifically. It was an important and necessary move that started in the Renaissance; we had to dethrone the old, incredibly complex and increasingly problematic model of the universe, the one with the earth at the center and rotating and counter-rotating spheres with stars stuck into them. The old model was collapsing under the weight of irreconcilable new data from new and better telescopes. A handful of very bright people, Tycho Brahe and Nicolaus Copernicus among them, kicked the old model and it fell apart, to be replaced by something that made elegant sense of the data: a sun-centered universe that (we now know) is afloat in an unimaginable sea of galaxies and stars. The old "poetic" truth in this case wasn't poetic at all. It was a manmade mess.

"Real science" was off and running. It has run and run, and we have learned so much: about the minute caperings of electrons and the pairing of ions, the union of atoms into molecules and molecules into macromolecules, up to the enormous twining chains of nucleotides that tell a cell what to make and how to make it, the cell itself included. We have learned much about what life does, and such knowledge is almost too marvelous for us. We have learned much, too, at the opposite end of the scale, the cosmic level, where galaxies skitter at unimaginable speeds and stars flare and collapse.

But there are other truths, truths of the heart and soul. Science has never been particularly good at coping with them, although it has sometimes tried. We still don't know much about the mind's working or what drives the human heart. We've tried all sorts of models of psychology, and they still routinely fall apart. Worse still, when we try the science gets soggy—not because scientists aren't trying their best, but because nature and nurture stubbornly refuse to be teased apart—and the prose gets flaccid. What makes us tick? How can we understand ourselves?

The poet W. B. Yeats wrote of going down into the "foul rag-and-bone shop of the heart"—a deep poetic truth, that. To understand yourself, to reach the place of authentic speaking, you must first delve into your own darkness. You must face your own shadow and accept it as truly yours.

There's truth and then there's deep truth, and they are not the same. Scientists know this; they firmly declare that there are whole areas of knowledge they have no intention of trying to tackle because the scientific method doesn't work there. It has enough trouble with simple biology, after all. (The first law of biology is, "Under precisely controlled laboratory conditions, living creatures will do as they damn well please.")

Meanwhile, somewhere over in the next county, the Biblical inerrantists are slugging it out with their opposite numbers. The fight is about factual truth. Is the Bible factually true, or isn't it? If it contains a single factual error, does that invalidate the whole she-bang? What about its logical inconsistencies, which are legion? Both sides of this debate are somewhat behind the times, in that in this postmodern era facts are now deeply out of fashion. It's too easy to conflate a fact with a cultural assumption; we do it all the time. To see every word of Scripture as literally true is to ignore the fact that it's all in translation, and all translations are only approximate, because they invariably involve translators' having to make choices.

Sometimes, regarding the battle over Scriptural inerrancy, I feel almost as though I'm back in that time right before Brahe and Copernicus, back when scholars and philosophers saw the universe as rotating around the Earth. To make this work, they had to create an elaborate system of interlocking spheres rotating against each other—a large, fragile, top-heavy model, erected more from the old human need to avoid saying "Sorry, got that wrong" than from observation of what the thing is really doing. In the end, the model fell apart with a single well-aimed kick.

But both sides of the battle miss out on something extremely important: a thing doesn't have to be literally true to be really true. Sidney's poem isn't about cardiac co-transplants, especially given that the poem was written in the late sixteenth century; it's about love, and especially about the sort of self-giving love that inextricably blends two human lives. Yeats's poem has nothing to do with real ladders, not even about real wrong-doing or horrible intentions or anything of that order; it has to do with our capacity for ignoring our own shadow side. These are truths of the first order. Who cares whether or not they're facts?

Would my faith collapse if I learned, to my absolute certainty, that the so-called facts of Christianity—the Virgin Birth and the Resurrection—were not literally true? Obviously, it's not likely to happen; the Virgin Birth is pretty much unprovable one way or the other, and neither history nor archaeology is apt to have the necessary incontrovertible evidence to disprove the Resurrection. But truly, I could live in my faith even if the facts proved to be not literally factual. They would still represent, for me, great truths: that God chose to become human, and that God's power and purpose is, in the long run, far greater than any mere death we can throw against it.

I imagine this is true for people of all faiths and times, that what matters aren't the facts—if facts there are, given postmodernism and the Heisenberg uncertainty principle—but instead the deep insights that poetry and myth convey, insights that tell the truths of the human heart. If there is no meaning to things, as some claim, then we can dispense with poetic truth. They can choose that road if they like. It's not one I find appealing.

Is my poetic truth delusional? I have no firm way of knowing. Does it matter to me, the vision I have of a life to come on the other side of death? Profoundly. Is it true? I think so, but if I'm wrong, I'm wrong. No way of finding out in this life, not for sure.

Is poetic truth the same as literal truth? Of course not. Is it shallower truth or deeper truth? Deeper, I think, and I hold up the Sidney poem as my witness. There are mere facts, not nearly as firm and incontrovertible as we once thought they were, and they can be as hard and fickle as the stones on a shingle beach—definite, yes, but turning treacherously under your foot. Then there are great truths, which are not necessarily literal truths. They may sink and yield under your foot, but they won't ever let you down.

✣ The Gray Man ✣

Contrary to what you might believe, book signings are no fun unless you're a big-time author—and even in that case I suspect it's still no fun; you just get a lot more attention. But I was not a big-time author, and the location of the book signing couldn't have been more inauspicious, given what I write about. I was at a bookstore in downtown Ottawa at noontime in March. Downtown Ottawa tends to be awash in baby boomer federal civil servants and businessthingies, who are not exactly receptive to the kind of classic Christian stuff that's my stock in trade. There may be—in fact, certainly there are—thoughtful inquirers in faith in those office buildings, but the predominant downtown Ottawa culture is apt to keep them operating well below the radar.

Although the bookstore was crawling with customers, few of them picked up my poor baby book and scanned the back cover, and those that did mostly put the book back down very quickly, as though it might bite them if riled. I think we sold four copies; something like that anyway. Fortunately, my Christian side knows that my authorial ego needs to be kept pruned way back, so I could be fairly philosophical about the whole business.

The lunch-hour crowd had thinned out, and I was just starting to think about folding up my tent and stealing quietly away, when a gray-haired, gray-faced man in a gray suit came up to the table. As I had done over and over for the previous hour-and-some, I made eye contact with him and smiled in what I hoped was a friendly, inviting way—with a face like mine, I'm never quite sure if that's what comes across, or if I just look faintly demented. He picked up the book, read the back cover, and actually *opened the book and read a little bit of it.* Then he put it down and announced, with the air of someone ready for a fight, "I'm really interested in spirituality, but I don't have any use at all for organized religion."

Sigh.

He then proceeded to lecture me on the misdeeds of the Christian church through the past couple of thousand years, as though he were conveying to me information I clearly lacked—if I could believe in this Christianity stuff, I must be completely ignorant of history. I did not tell him that I have a B.A. in European history, with a particular interest in the seventeenth century, one of the most religiously messy periods in all of modern history. (I've always believed that eighteenth-century European rationalism was a gut response to the Thirty Years' War, but that's another essay.) When he paused, triumphant, I made my stock responses: first, that Christendom is not quite the same thing as Christianity, and that Christendom is pretty much dead these days, thanks be to God; and second, that blaming Christ for the sins of the Christian church is rather like holding Karl Marx accountable for Stalin. I don't think he'd thought about that one before.

The fact is that people in all places and times are subject to fits of bad behavior, and they're always looking to justify (or at least ignore) their own bad behavior, so they take something good or at least morally neutral, like God or natural selection, give it a good twist, and turn it into something with which to beat up other people. It almost doesn't matter what the raw material is—except that hatred done in the name of love is far more offensive than hatred done in the name of hatred. (I once came across an e-mail signature that read "And Jesus said: You did *what* in My name???")

All I can say is that those of us who are practicing Christians have to keep practicing because we haven't got it right yet, and we probably never will in this life, although some of us seem to be born with more grace, or have worked at it harder, than others. But we *know* we don't get it right. That's not God's fault, or Christ's, or even Christianity's. It's ours. Any belief worth its salt is not easy going, and we fall down on the path or go charging into the bramble patches because of our own wounds, our own anger or pride or self-righteousness, our own very human failings. It's sin—a word now out of fashion, but still so badly needed.

The man went on to tell me that he and his wife were "into" Aboriginal spirituality, one of the trendier ways of trying to be "a spiritual person" without actually believing anything. To my Aboriginal friends, this is something between ridiculous and offensive. I have listened to Mohawk and Algonquin grandmothers, to Miqma'q elders, to a Gwi'chin Anglican priest in her beaded stole and moccasins. I have joined in the smudge and the prayers at the opening of First Nations conferences. I have prayed and received the sacrament in an Ojibwa Roman Catholic church, where the altar covering was beautifully beaded deerskin. From what all of these people have told me, they have very definite beliefs; they do believe strongly in their Creator and the Creator's love for Creation. They have, as we do, ceremonies, disciplines, and wonderfully woven stories that represent and nourish their spirituality. The ones I've talked to also have few problems with my Christianity. They have huge problems with Christendom—with the abusive use of Christianity by European oppressors—but not with Christ himself. Many have themselves accepted Christ; others simply say that we are seeing different parts of the same rainbow.

I listened to the gray man as politely as I could (something of a strain when a person is patronizing me) without getting into an argument, because we both had views that weren't about to change. I understood his; I don't think he wanted to understand mine. Eventually he realized what time it was and headed back to his office, and I packed my books and left the store.

A couple of months after the book signing, I read a newspaper essay by a noted Canadian sci-fi writer, Spider Robinson. It was a blistering attack on theistic religions (Judaism, Christianity, Islam). He rejects God as being "a bearded paranoid in the sky who enjoys having His feet regularly washed in the blood of heathens and then licked clean, and who plans to torture most humans for eternity." Buddhism, on the other hand, he thinks is wonderful, full of built-in toleration and seeking only to be free from delusion. When I relayed this to a Buddhist nun I know, she burst out laughing and said, "Does he think that there were no Buddhists in the Japanese Army in World War II?" She went on, more seriously: "What people do is take everything negative and hand it over to 'organized religion'—by which they mean Christianity and maybe Islam—and they take all the good stuff and hand it over to 'spirituality.' And that's just plain inaccurate."

As someone (I don't know who) once said, "Everybody's got a theology; the question is whether it's any good." That is, everyone has *some* belief about God. This "bearded paranoid" God image is really lousy theology, used as a weapon in the writer's gripe with the Christian church; like most lousy theology it is used to beat people up. It makes me want to yell, "Will you *please* stop hitting me over the head for my beliefs when you don't have a clue what they are because you refuse to listen to them in the first place?" When someone snipes at my faith as naïve and self-deluding, I find myself saying, "OK, but I've got Johann Sebastian Bach in my corner, and do you *really* believe that man was a fool?" Being attacked for my beliefs by someone who hasn't troubled to find out *what* I believe does tend to make me a little cranky.

I cannot speak for other traditions, only for my own, but when I look at the great world religions I see elements in common. There is something higher and better to aspire to. We must struggle honestly with the here-and-now of sin and suffering. We must show compassion and love for others. We require discipline and work to pursue the Way (and it is a Way, not an arrival). Our theologies differ, and each of us holds to the one that makes the most sense to us, but we respect the other's truth, as we hope the other will respect ours. As Paul said, "Now we see in a mirror, dimly, but then we shall see face to face. Now I know only in part; then I shall know fully, even as I have been fully known."

There is a point to this organized religion bit: it involves community, connectedness in space and time, and the requirement that we answer to our fellow believers for the belief choices we make—for that accountability is the flip side of the freedom to choose.

Still, the gray man represents quite a large group in North American society, the people who say they do want spirituality but don't want religion. As though the two are somehow antithetical. But they aren't. It may be possible, I suppose, to hold vague content-free spiritual beliefs that require no action, but I don't know how well that can persist over time, or what good it could do a person in any sort of trouble. If you believe, you have at least a vague notion *what* you believe in; the question is whether you've examined those beliefs and their implications, and what you're prepared to do with them.

Both the sci-fi writer and the gray man have rejected Christianity because some of its followers were (and still are) hypocrites—people whose walk and talk seem to have nothing to do with each other. But they commit both bad history and bad theology by saying that this is *all* Christianity has done, and that Christianity's errors reflect a nasty-minded God-person. Idealizing another group (Aboriginal peoples or Buddhists) is also bad history, and it fails to respect the humanity and imperfection of the other.

Spirituality is what tugs the soul Godward, as a heliotrope turns its flowers and leaves sunward, or one magnet tugs at another. But what if you want to take God out of the equation? You can't, really. All you can do is to paste a "not-God" label onto God, or (as the sci-fi writer did) paste an ugly manmade demon face over God's face—as if by calling God something other than God you could get away from God's centrality as the source of all goodness.

Can you be a spiritual person without organized religion? What's organized religion? There are the institutions, of course, which are booming in parts of this world and apparently dying back in other parts. They are as human as their members, and each has its particular shadow side, although at their best they conserve and pass on tradition and community that we would be quite wrong to toss out with the garbage. But a religion worth its salt is much more than that; it's a set of beliefs, practices, and moral judgments with considerable coherence, all based (or so we hope) on the goodness of love.

Spirituality and religion aren't antithetical; quite the opposite. Spirituality is like milk and religious belief and practice are like the milk jug; without the milk, the jug is dry, empty of nourishment or refreshment, and pretty much pointless. But without the jug the milk runs all over the table.

Could I have said this to the gray man, or could I have written this to the sci-fi writer? I don't know. I detected a lot of anger in both of them, passive aggression in the gray man and open hostility in the writer. I don't get into arguments with people with a big chip on their shoulder because it's a bit like trying to teach a pig to sing; it's a waste of my time, and it irritates the pig.

Does God love them both? Absolutely. I am sure in my bones that when they cross the River (as we all must, sooner or later) and find themselves lovingly cupped in the palm of God's hand, they will be in for a delightful surprise.

❧ Needful Things ☙

I saw the letter carrier's head bobbing past my front windows as he strode across my lawn to the letter box. Mail's here. I keep hoping to get the moonstone cross that I'd bought from eBay, but no such luck this morning. Every single damned thing in the box was a bill or trouble.

The car insurance, specifically. It's a long story and not worth bothering about, but the car insurance renewal led into all sorts of down-the-line need-to-do things that I didn't especially want to do, stuff I find stressful at the best of times, and these are not the best of times. I plowed through the mess, hating every minute of it but knowing it was mine to do and there's no point putting it off. Very Lenten.

We know, on a purely practical level, that the bills have to get paid on time, or reasonably so, that the garbage has to be put out and the cats taken for their shots and that time must be spent in the dentist's chair, because otherwise the consequences are unpleasant. So we do the needful things, even when we'd much rather be doing something else, because that's part of living life in this world as an adult, which is what this world expects us to be. Straightforward enough; it's a matter of operating responsibly in the real world.

But then there's a whole different layer of things-to-do that we think are less urgent, or that we shy away from, because the consequences aren't quite so obvious, or because the consequences won't necessarily fall on us (or not nearly soon enough). Or because we fail to see them as needful in the first place. Yes, I know in theory that I need to lose this many pounds or else there's an increased chance of my dying of a heart attack. I just can't bring myself to care enough to do anything much about it, or not for any length of time anyway. You could make the case that it's my body and if I choose not to look after it, it's my choice—but my kids might think differently, and so might those (taxpayers, in Canada) who pay for my health care.

Moving deeper, it's the inner needful things, the things of the soul, that are (sadly) the easiest of all to skip and the most central of all to our ultimate well-being. It's terribly easy to slip into minor self-dishonesty, cheap-claiming this virtue or that instead of doing the hard work of actually building it. We claim to be loving, but we don't act that way. We claim to be strong when in fact we're weak, and we have no intention of doing anything about our weakness. We claim to be mature when we're just selfish children, still acting as though the playground rules apply. We want the credit; we want to feel good about ourselves. But we don't want the work. Or we're too scared by it; we're already defeated by the very idea of it, overwhelmed by the unspoken knowledge of all the problems we've turned away from for all those years.

We want others to see us not as we are but as we wish to be seen, disregarding all the stuff we really don't want to do anything about. We want others to take us at our own evaluation, however inflated.

They can't. Not for long, anyway. Our actions disillusion them and they turn away. The mask looks more and more like a mask, and less and less like a warm human face. Few people are satisfied with masks, at least in the long run.

We can be real people, honest with ourselves and with others, or we can decompose ourselves into persona and shadow—the good-looking bits over here, on display to ourselves and the world, and the not-so-good-looking bits over there, just behind and a little to the right, where we don't have to see them, and where they can get up to all sorts of trouble behind our back.

This is the great gift of Christianity: the expectation that we will be honest with ourselves as far as we possibly can, because only in honesty can we be truly loving. If you can't see and love your own self, how can you possibly love anyone else?

This is what Lent is for; this is why Christians welcome it with open arms instead of turning away from it. Lent is the time for the soul's needful things, beginning with honesty—real honesty, the sort that looks around the soul's entire landscape (not just the pretty bits) and compares what it sees to what the Christ taught. No, I cannot turn away from the poor, enjoying my wealth, and speak well of myself as a Christian. No, I cannot claim to be loving when in fact I act out of self-centeredness. No, I cannot pass cheap-and-easy judgment on another and claim immunity from being judged myself. No, I cannot use others as sexual things and see it as no big deal. No, I cannot write off another human soul on sheer gut dislike and still think of myself as a nice person. No, I cannot impose my needs upon others without meeting their needs in return.

Changing these patterns *is* needful, because they shape our souls, and we must answer to God for the soul choices we have made, and for what our soul choices have done to the people in our lives. That particular reckoning will come, inevitably, when we face our Creator and give account of our lives.

I didn't enjoy the afternoon, but I did get a sense of (rather grim) satisfaction that at least I was getting these needful things dealt with, little as I wanted to. I got the insurance problems on the way to being sorted out. Then I made a cup of mocha and sat down by the window, looking out into the gray street, and did needful work with my own gray lump of anger.

🌺 Hide and Seek 🌺

It was an extremely silly game the kids used to play when they were little. A child would stand out in plain sight—say, in the middle of the living room carpet—and would cover his face with his hands and chant ceremonially "You'll never *find* me!" Even when the child in question was less than three feet tall, this was clearly a bit of ironic nonsense. Whatever their failings, my children are not fools, and their sense of humor developed early. (I knew I was doing something right when my younger cub, at the impossibly cute age of four, stuck a lollipop in his mouth and snarled "So long, sucker!")

Yet it happens. It's not just a little kid's joke; it's a pattern of adult behavior, and a troubling one. We do stuff that we know, in our deepest hearts, is wrong and is going to get us in trouble sooner or later, and we stand in the middle of the living room carpet with our hands over our eyes chanting ceremonially "You'll never *find* me!"—the you in question being (say) the IRS or Revenue Canada, or the bishop, or the boss, or the spouse, or the press, or the children, or (above all) God. We fail. We know we fail. We even understand, perhaps, why it is we fail; we fail because we're human and sinners and all that—and yet we clap our hands over our eyes, hoping that nobody will ever notice.

The problem is that they *do* see us—other people, for starters. Sooner or later, the auditors *are* going to want to see the books. We hope that by futzing around with the accounting we can hide what we've done, but in fact the more we try the more we convince them that something's going on. We're standing there with our hands over our face chanting "They'll never *find* me!"

We can try to divert their attention, perhaps by blaming another person. Choose a scapegoat, load all the dysfunction on her back, and drive her out into the wilderness, chanting "It's all her fault!" This way, they'll be so focused on what she's done wrong that they won't notice what we've been up to. Maybe we really believe that by doing so the wrong will truly go away and we'll be fine again. Or if someone questions what we've been up to, we can shut the person up by direct personal attacks to his face or behind his back, or (even better) both. Shoot the messenger: it's a pattern as old and as common as dirt.

Then there's good old denial. We can even make our own minds fail to see the problem, perhaps by focusing on what good things we've done or by telling ourselves that the ends justify the means. We can set up idols of one sort or another and prove to ourselves that these gods were God and that by serving them we were doing God's work. There are a thousand ways in which we can hide our eyes from our own transgressions. Some of them actually work. For a while.

The problem is that there is One from whom nothing we do is ever hidden. As the psalmist said,

> You know when I sit down and when I rise up;
> you discern my thoughts from far away.
> You search out my path and my lying down,
> and are acquainted with all my ways.

Even before a word is on my tongue.
O Lord, you know it completely.
—PSALM 139:2–4

The One knows that we all fall short of the mark and screw up, that we do wrong and sometimes don't repent of it. The One loves us, whatever we've done. But sometimes we have to admit to ourselves and to God that we've really blown it. It wasn't just a little-bitty booboo; it was real *wrong,* a really bad decision or a pattern we should never have fallen into, not just a minor mistake. We shouldn't have done it, and the wrong has consequences that we (and most likely others) are going to have to live with. One of those consequences is that we're not going to feel particularly good about ourselves, and we're probably going to lose face in the eyes of our peers. Our egotism is going to take a beating, which is something we all fear deeply.

But as St. Thérèse of Lisieux said, in her gentle way, "If you are willing to serenely bear the trial of being displeasing to yourself, then you will be for Jesus a pleasant place of shelter." We grow our souls, and grow them strong and healthy, by accepting the fact that we're flawed, we make mistakes, we have to admit those mistakes to ourselves, God, and others, and we must be willing to made amends and let God set us to rights.

We have been given the gift of the knowledge of good and evil in all its terror and beauty. We have, in the Gospels, been given the Kingdom Way, and we know when we follow it and when we turn away and charge off in the opposite direction—or if we don't, we can't claim to be followers of the Christ, however often we warm the pews. We can't stand in the middle of the living room carpet playing games any more.

God will gently take our hands, pull them away from our face, and look us right in the eye, with love and understanding, but also with insight and justice. No matter how hard we try to pretend to ourselves, our God will always find us. Why, if we believe that God is love, should this frighten us so badly?

❧ Half a Moon ☙

It was so vivid that, for a moment, I had trouble concentrating on the highway instead of the sky—not a good idea, driving out from the city on a fall Friday night, when unchancy critters are just waiting to get themselves flattened by passing vehicles. But when I got off at my exit, there it was again: the moon. I couldn't take time to stop, but I got a good look anyway.

The moon was about a day past half-full and slung low in the sky. Something about the angle to the earth made its light unusually vivid, its shape exceptionally full and strong. If this were a full moon, you'd be able to read by it.

The evening was a bit cloudy, surrounding the moon's face with a gentle halo. Maybe it was those wisps of cloud; maybe it was an optical illusion, something about the angle, the unusual brilliance, but I could have sworn that I saw the dark of the moon outlined, rounding out the half-moon into a whole. Nah, couldn't be. It was one of those things like the spots you see if you look at a bright light, some trick of ocular processing. You can't really see the dark side of the moon, not unless you're an astronomer, and certainly not out here and under these conditions. There's no light bouncing off it, after all.

But still, there was the illusion. Maybe when we expect a full circle, we see one; the brain completes what the eye desires. Of course, the brain is right: the opposite curve, the unseen face, does exist even if all I see of it is illusory.

I thought of the opposite illusion, the one that happens in daylight. The moon can be hanging there as a wisp of light in the sky, so apparently frail that you feel you could reach up and pinch right through it with thumb and forefinger; the wisp would be cool, damp, and utterly insubstantial. Those thunderheads off to the west, on the other hand, look splendidly massive, solid as cliff faces. Yet the reality is the opposite.

Which is the illusion? I have no proof one way or another. But I have my ways of suspecting.

The moon reminded me that I know, and don't know, God. I know God most directly through Jesus and through the communion of saints—the testimony of those, living and dead, through whom God has clearly spoken. But I also know God indirectly, through hints and suggestions, as astronomers can discern an unseen planet through the wobbles in other planets' orbits.

I can suspect God, the way I suspect the dark side of the moon, through Creation: not because it's neat and orderly, the work of a master planner, but because it's so bloody *creative*— messy, real, outrageous, full of loose ends and oddities and Mac-Gyverings (the pit of the avocado, the jury-rigging of the panda's thumb), just the way all creativity is. If this universe is ever to be a neat and tidy place, it will be so only at the very end, I suspect, rather like sewing the loose ends of yarn into a handknit sweater just after you put it together.

I can suspect God, like the dark side of the moon, in the persistence of human love. What makes us rise to a crisis with altruism? Don't give me the selfish-DNA argument; it's such an anti-Hobson's choice "solution" as to make a logician barf. I have seen people *in extremis* reach out to comfort others, finding comfort themselves in giving it. You can try to argue love away as a sociobiological adaptation; but couldn't it just as easily (more easily?) be gravitational pull?

Above all, I suspect God in the iridescence of paradox and mystery, the colors that won't resolve themselves into simple pink or purple but vibrate so with light that you can't easily label them— or if you label the pink, you'll find yourself jumped by the purpleness and the other way around. Deep truth, even if fictional, is truer than the shallow truth of provable factoids. Is the Virgin Birth a literal truth? Mystery says, "That's asking the wrong question."

I know that I don't know. I know the other half of the moon is there; I think I can discern it, but I know I can't see it. I see God only as through a glass, darkly; I can sense the fullness and completeness of God, but I know that I know so little and will probably never know much more than this on this side of the River.

How, then, could I ever claim to be in possession of the truth, and to judge others for their adherence to that truth? We outgrew it a long, long time ago, when we started to suspect that truth is a whole lot bigger than humankind can get its tiny mind around—and that there are mountains on the other side of the moon that we cannot see unaided. Not yet; not with these eyes, or in this life. The next, of course, is another matter.

CHAPTER 4

Answered Prayers

In you, O Lord, I take refuge;
let me never be put to shame.
In your righteousness deliver me
and rescue me;
incline your ear to me and
save me.
Be to me a rock of refuge,
a strong fortress to save me,
for you are my rock and
my refuge.

—PSALM 71:1–3

❧ Maya ❧

Ask, and it will be given you; search, and you will
find; knock, and the door will be opened for you.
For everyone who asks receives, and everyone who
searches finds, and for everyone who knocks, the door
will be opened. Is there anyone among you who,
if your child asks for bread, will give a stone?
Or if the child asks for a fish, will give a snake?
If you then, who are evil, know how to give good gifts
to your children, how much more will your Father
in heaven give good things to those who ask him?
—MATTHEW 7:7–11

You can't always get what you want.
—ROLLING STONES

You hear things in the frozen food aisle or waiting in line at the
bank; you pick stuff up by osmosis, I swear, if you live in a very
small town. I didn't know Maya at all well, but I knew the basics.
I knew she was in her early thirties, small and plumpish, with a
round, pretty face and a mass of russet curls. I knew that she was
married to Dan, a young bank manager, and that the two of them
had four young sons, the most recent only a few months old. I
knew that she hung out with our local Pentecostal Christian
group. I knew she had a really pretty old brick house with a garden
that was clearly her pride and joy.

Now, in the frozen food aisle, I was hearing about her cancer. A whisper here, a rumor there.

The same thing had hit a friend of mine, a few years earlier, and I gather it isn't uncommon: in some women, the huge hormonal whammies associated with having a baby trigger a particularly aggressive form of breast cancer. My friend went through hellish treatment, but she beat her disease; now, fifteen years later, she's still cancer-free.

But Maya's cancer had gotten away from them. It leapt free of control, and now it was moving like fire through dry, long grass.

I heard the whispers around town for several weeks before I got the phone call. It was Angelique, asking if I'd like to be a member of a prayer group that was going to surround Maya with the healing power of prayer. I like Angelique, but some of what she was saying made me nervous. This wasn't a group that was wrapping Maya in support and comfort; this was a group of prayer warriors who were determined to beat this thing. They wanted, Angelique told me, only people who were 100 percent sure that God would provide a miracle. They couldn't afford doubt. Doubt would undermine the prayer power.

I told Angelique that I'd certainly pray for Maya and her family, but I didn't think I could manage the prayer-warrior bit. I could almost hear her thinking "Anglicans! Humph!" as we wound up the conversation.

So I prayed for Maya. I think most people in town did. Maya's house was full of people praying big-time, men and women, young and old, prayer warriors in no doubt whatsoever that God would provide the miracle she needed. They prayed fervently night and day, constantly surrounding her. Anyone who expressed the slightest doubt about her prospects for a complete cure was out of the house.

They prayed and prayed as she shriveled, weakened and struggled with the pain. They prayed when she slipped into a coma. They were still praying, still certain of a miracle, even after her breath ceased and her skin began to cool.

Their faith in prayer was so strong, so certain, so complete, that nobody had taken her kids aside and prepared them for their mother's death.

That would have been doubt, you see, and doubt would block the miracle.

Maya's death shook up a whole lot of devout Christians in our community. They'd been so certain of the power of prayer, so convinced that as long as prayer was pure enough, faith certain enough, belief sufficiently absolute, Maya would be made well. God had promised that prayer would be granted.

They forgot that people prayed with just as much conviction and fervor while they were trundled into the gas chambers at Auschwitz.

They forgot that Jesus prayed with passion and desperation in the dark garden, the night before the soldiers came to get him.

They forgot what he ended his prayer with: "Yet your will, not mine, be done."

I do not believe that God willed Maya to die. I believe that her cancer was the result of plain old biology: probably a genetic predisposition, kickstarted by all those potent hormones, and once an aggressive cancer gets going it's really something of a crap shoot whether you're going to be able to catch it and cure it before it takes off and kills you. My friend was exceptionally lucky; Maya was not.

I do not believe that an early death from cancer was in God's plan for Maya, or that losing their mother was in God's plans for her children, or that losing his wife was in God's plan for Dan. I do sometimes have to ask whether God has plans for us at all. If

God does indeed plan all this stuff for us, one individual at a time, then God has got to be a bit of a sadist, and I have real trouble with a God like that.

I do believe that miracles (in the sense of inexplicable cures) do sometimes happen. I have another friend who was diagnosed with non-Hodgkin's lymphoma, and the disease simply vanished, a day before she was due to go into hospital for surgery. It's never come back, and it's been more than twenty years.

I do not believe that we can buy miracles. They happen or they don't happen, but they cannot be forced.

I do believe in the power of prayer. It is, however, my experience that prayer may take you to places you never expected to visit instead of the places you wanted to get to, and that a frustrated human will can be a terrible thing.

I do agree with the Rolling Stones: you can't always get what you want.

But most of all, I believe in the terribly treacherous power of magical thinking. I believe in it most profoundly, for I know how easily I fall into it myself.

It rests on a basis of sound kindergarten thinking. If I am good, good things will happen to me; if I am bad, bad things will happen to me. It rests on the assumption that God is the Big Daddy who can be wheedled and persuaded and who will make things happen by direct divine intervention. This thinking rests on Bible verses, yanked out of context and taken literally and uncritically as the truth. It rests on a highly selective approach to the data: we will consider only those cases, like my friend with the non-Hodgkin's lymphoma, in which something that looks miraculous *did* happen, and not the cases in which, for all the praying and all the love and sincerity, the patient died. We will close our eyes to the possibility that it won't come out the way we want it to. We will act blindly, without thinking about what we're really doing—which is playing mind games with God. Bargaining. Looking for the old quid pro quo. *Tell you what, God, let's do a deal here. I'll believe absolutely in You, and you make Maya well, OK?*

I'm not making fun of this, honest. I'm seeing it from the inside, for I have done this myself, any number of times, usually with disastrous results. I think perhaps just about everyone (except perhaps the real saints, of whom I am not one) does the same thing. It's bred into our very bones; we can't help it: I want. I need. Suffering is bad and shouldn't happen to me. I want to live and to be happy and to belong and be loved and have someone to watch over me, and have my needs met, and live pain-free to an advanced old age and then die without suffering in my sleep. This is what we all want, because we're human, and because it is what we want it is what we ask God to give us.

Too often, though, it doesn't work out that way. I refuse to believe that God intends things to go wrong, but this is a world in which those three wild cards—biology, physics, and human psychology—are all still very much in the game. It wasn't God's will that caused Maya's cancer; it was biology. Pure and simple. Just as it was physics, pure and simple, that tumbled the Iranian city of Bam, killing some twenty-seven thousand people, men and women, babies and small children, the elderly, sinners and saints, most of them if not completely innocent then certainly not worthy of being horribly killed in a moment's seismic shudder. The fervent prayers of relatives and seekers did not bring the dead safely out from under the rubble of their homes.

That isn't what prayer does. At least not in my experience.

I know of another woman who died of cancer surrounded by her church family. She died long before I heard of her, but her memory, and the memory of her dying, still lit up the landscape, years later.

Felicia also had young children when the cancer came to claim her. She'd had it before, one of the more aggressive skin cancers, but they thought they'd gotten it under control. It came back when her son was six and her daughter was four, and this time (as in Maya's) it jumped the fence and spread.

Her community closed in around her, with prayer for her healing, but also with realism. When, after failed chemotherapy, it became clear that her cancer was mortal, they closed in with love, support, and practical common sense. They wrapped her in palliative care. They also wrapped her husband and children in love and support. There were long, tearful, loving talks at the kitchen table. The kids talked, cried, and were held and listened to. There were casseroles and cool drinks, help with the pain meds, support with the doctors' appointments.

There was prayer, not of the prayer-warrior type but a gentle and constant wrapping-around. Felicia and her family were clothed in a blanket of prayer, gently and warmly. Community knit itself together around them and found joy in gentle service. When she slipped into a coma, it was as though they'd laid her lovingly in a small boat and set the boat free to glide down a river to a new and glorious shore; there was grief, to be sure, but there were also smiles, for she was free of pain now, and safe, and rejoicing in the palm of her Creator's hand. She had passed from life into Life.

The community wrapped itself around her husband and kids, sat with them through their mourning, and supported them in the days that followed. The community was still there, still bonded together through the experience, years after Felicia died. Prayer formed community and it witnessed to God's love. It bore Felicia and her family through their experience as something memorably beautiful, instead of pounding on God's door and insisting on one particular result.

This, I do believe, is what prayer is meant to do.

We don't get closer to God through magical thinking; we get closer to God through real trust, and through the belief that God will bring all things to right in the end. Which doesn't mean it will turn out the way we want it to tomorrow.

"Yet your will, not mine, be done." I don't see this as passive acceptance of whatever life hands us to deal with. I do believe that sometimes we're called into active (if peaceful) resistance, standing up to human evil. But I also believe that we pray in trust, not in magical thinking, and trust is sometimes a long-run business.

Maybe the point of this passage from Matthew is to remind us that whatever the results are—whether we get what we ask for or not—the essential point of prayer is what it makes of us. The journey, not the arrival, matters, to quote Leonard Woolf. Sometimes we stand there, yelling *"Where are you?"* at a God who feels very far away. We pound on that closed door with both fists, yelling *"Help me!"* We sit in silent despair, hearing only silence. But it's in this very tough, very human way that we learn to sit with suffering in ourselves and in others, and that is the path of Love. That's the Kingdom way.

Those prayer warriors years ago were holding out for that thousand-dollar bill of a miraculous healing. And so they deprived themselves and Maya and her family of a thousand one-dollar bills of daily comfort, the small change of love that so enriched Felicia's latter days. It was too bad.

Pray to God with everything you've got. Accept that you don't always get what you want—but remember that the end result of your prayer may be infinitely more than you can ask for or imagine.

❧ Two Pieces in Mud Season ❧

Where I live, in southeastern Ontario, we have not one season but at least six and possibly seven, to wit: spring, summer, fall, mud season, winter (high and low), and mud season redux. The two mud seasons are preparatory inter-seasons, times when the landscape cools down for winter or begins, with what feels like infinite slowness, to warm up for spring.

Mud season actually only lasts for six to eight weeks, but it can feel endless—particularly spring mud season, because by that time we're all so totally fed up after winter. It can also be terribly hard on the soul, since the landscape is dun and gray and the weather tends to be overcast but uneventful.

But I have long since realized that mud season, properly considered, does have its virtues. Sometimes we need to be held in a space of quietness and non-event, a time of preparation. Mud season is a substantial vote against the "fun right now!" values shouted by the media and popular culture. It is a witness to slowness, groundedness, and living with the moment, however unlovely the moment may seem. It begs for patience, a virtue most of us need to cultivate anyway, and for a richer understanding of how this earth really works. So I've learned to treasure mud season—at least occasionally. When I get fed up with it, I find there's usually some God-Stuff lurking under last fall's leaves, if I'm willing to look.

Here are two bits from spring mud season.

1. Time

I am sure that somewhere, possibly in the Smithsonian or some other highly respected institution, there resides a clock that ticks the days precisely, each second exactly measured and tabulated. To this clock each second is exactly the length of that second, each day's count of seconds and minutes and hours duly recorded, with allowances being made for slight natural irregularities in the turn of the Earth or her orbit around the Sun. Time, to this clock, is a steady procession, as well defined and amenable to measure as a finely chiseled chunk of granite, as definite as diamond.

But to the soul, time doesn't work like that. It's not definite and adamantine; it's more like yarn, or perhaps even Silly Putty, stretching out or contracting depending on what's going on. In spring mud season, for example, time stretches out in a sagging wobbly loop, stretches almost to breaking point sometimes. Each hour seems day-long; each day seems to go on for a week. This is because we are all fed up to the hind teeth with Canadian winter and we want spring and we want it *now*. But it isn't now. It isn't for at least a couple-three more weeks, with any luck. Until then, it's mud season.

I wonder if it felt thus to Jesus in the desert—that each day of hunger and loneliness, each night of cold, seemed endlessly extended, time stretching out until it sagged. I'd like to believe he was too close to God to notice, that instead of time dragging along it whipped by as he walked in companionship with his Abba. I know how time can stop altogether at rare moments, and then you know that you are with your Creator and wish only to be there for eternity. I imagine this is what Jesus experienced. I wish I could be that way too—so wrapped up in my Creator that such irritants as cold rain and whippy winds are irrelevant, or at least tolerable in the certainty of glory. But that's not where I am right now. So time stretches, and the mud season days feel long.

But looking back, I find a pattern that is profoundly comforting. I can remember any number of mud seasons; we have two a year after all, and they add up. I can remember any number of periods of suffering, if I flip back through the calendar. I know now that with healing I can revisit how I felt in those fits of anger or suffering or grief. But although I can remember in full detail, with the color of recollected emotion, I find I can't really revisit those times in any immediate sense. They used to own me; now they don't. I can't (and wouldn't want to if I could) re-enter the experience and *be* there. With real healing, suffering, like mud season, finally gets left behind.

What I can remember with immediacy and vividness are other moments, moments of blessedness. I can remember moments that, as I was in them, I wrapped carefully in memory and stowed away, like wrapping something in amber, so that I could pick them up and return to them fully whenever I wanted. Sitting with my first baby in the Public Gardens in Halifax; walking through the woods in the mountains I loved; standing in the kitchen being jumped by joy for no reason whatsoever. In these moments, time didn't stretch; it stopped altogether. A very different matter.

You can't arrange these moments; they simply arrive when it's possible to experience them, if you're willing to stop for them. There are times when, for whatever reason, they aren't on the possibility list. Too much stress, I find, and I'm going to do mud season-type time-stretching, not those flickers of pure eternity. Not because God isn't out there waiting to connect, but because I'm in no condition to entertain him.

Mud season is something that a person has to get through without whining too much, knowing that each day will end, and each day does bring you a little closer to spring, although it doesn't feel that way. It's easier to believe this about the season itself, because the calendar is reassuring and experience says that it really is only a matter of time.

It's harder to believe that the soul's mud season will end in time, and that joy does wait, especially if mud season has been going on for far too long. But as I tell myself over and over, it's only a matter of doing the work of healing and giving it time. Time may seem to stretch to threadlike extensibility in mud season, but it does pass. Time only stands still in joy.

2. Waiting
Dammit, I want *green.*

Yes, I know, I know. Look at any tree or shrub in the neighborhood and you'll see buds, emergent young leaves, the awkward dangle of tree flowers. The local willows have turned that peculiar pre-leaf bronzy chartreuse, and it's only May 1, which (in these parts) is a bit early for full leaf-out. I know. I've lived in Canada for more than thirty years now, and I should be used to this. There are places where it's worse. In Halifax, for example, spring doesn't happen until about 2:30 in the afternoon of May 29, and it lasts for about fifteen minutes. I know, because I timed it; when I went for my coffee break the city was still in late winter and when I came back, it was in full summer. Haligonians will tell you that I am not kidding.

But I still want green, and I want it now. Not next week, which is when we'll probably see it. *Now.* Instead, I see only what looks like the infinitely-stretching-out tail end of mud season, the trees still gray-brown against a sullen sky.

I think everybody feels more or less the same way around here. There's a sort of collective held breath as we wait for the shimmer of color to erupt overhead. People are out tentatively poking at their gardens, looking down the street, expectant yet hesitant. We don't think it's going to snow again, but we can't be absolutely sure. No point in planting anything yet, unless it's something hardy.

Christians feel the same way about the coming of the Kingdom—if they think about it at all. Many mainstream Christians hardly give the idea of the Second Coming a moment's thought, considering it the province of more adventurous believers, but we still say in the Eucharist "Christ has died; Christ is risen; Christ will come again." The earliest Christians believed that the Second Coming was imminent. But the wait has gone on so long that the prospect seems to stretch right over the horizon and into the indefinite future, for most of us at least. I don't know many Anglicans with bumper stickers saying "In case of Rapture, this car will be empty," which, in any event, seems just a little spiritually presumptuous for Anglican tastes. The world continues in its usual (and at the moment particularly dismal) ways. Hopes rise and fall, just as the seasons cycle. I know for sure that spring will come, but I know with equal certainty that the muggy heat of August will follow, and we'll cycle inevitably back into winter again. I wish I had the same certainty about the cycle of good and evil in this world, but sometimes mud season really does seem to stretch on for years.

We want God to speak up, to make big splashy miracles in order to prove to us that God really is in charge. We're sick of the bad guys getting away with it and the good guys (at least the ones we like, ourselves most especially included) not getting their just rewards. We want God to intervene actively, thrusting a stick in this world's endlessly spinning hamster wheel so that sinners will be stopped and tumble off, astonished and corrected. We want that Big Bang moment that justifies us as the good guys and proves that the ends did indeed justify the means we used, in spite of our own inner doubt and the criticism of others. We want God to establish, in sight of all our foes, who's right and who's wrong, and we want it *now.* Of course, we know where we stand in all this. I don't hear anyone calling for the Rapture who isn't totally sure that he or she will be raptured.

But Christians have been calling for the Second Coming since Paul was Saul, and it's been a long couple of millennia—an endless sort of mud season. At least at present, God does not seem to work this way, or not reliably (and what use is an unreliable God?) any more than God reliably intervenes with big, splendid miracles whenever devoutly requested. Is the problem God here, or is it our expectations? Are we, perhaps, looking for the wrong thing?

My neighbors and I are making a mistake in keeping our eyes on the trees overhead when we should be paying closer attention to the ditches. Because that's where the action is at the moment. Not at eye level or above, but underfoot. Look down, and you'll see something different: soft grasses emerging, the green bloom of mosses, tips of occasional weeds.

Yes, it still looks as though the world is going to hell in a handbasket, a viewpoint that goes back to Ancient Greece at the least and likely further back than that. Yes, we can point to reality TV, the decline of civility, and the rise of our culture's peculiarly narcissistic, trivial self-absorption, although I suspect that both have been around in other guises since human beings first stood upright. Certainly warfare has been part of the picture from the get-go, as have hunger and cruelty toward the helpless.

But something *has* changed, and it's changed underfoot: our expectations. The haunted eyes of starving infants now reach us through the media, and their humanity and suffering pierce our complacency. We have begun to take a look at the propriety of oppression, even if oppression still exists. We no longer shrug over the casualties of war. Their casualties have begun to matter to us, if not as much as our own; the deaths of our opponents are no longer a matter for rejoicing but for gravity. Maybe not for everyone yet, but for many, and more as time passes.

I don't know about the long run, of course; maybe the Rapture people are simply more long-sighted than I am. But in my lifetime, maybe the Kingdom coming will have nothing to do with bodies being snatched up or left behind; maybe it will be a rise in human consciousness, an acceptance of our need for love and our need to share it—God's love, always, but transmitted by human hands and voices. Not a matter of angels blowing trumpets and mighty battles between Good and Evil, but a quiet greening underfoot, so quiet that we may not even know it. Grace prevenient, going before us and preparing the way.

When I walked down to the village for the Saturday papers, the neighborhood trees still lifted bare branches against the jostling breeze, gray-brown in the dull late-morning light. But the grass under my feet was lush and verdant, and very, very green.

✿⁓ Driving Home ⁓✿

No doubt about it; it must be global warming. The weather continues to be about as wonky as I've ever seen it. Not only did we go from late summer to November without pausing at real fall, but for a while there we seemed to be skipping mud season altogether in favor of high winter, at least a month too early.

I realized this as I emerged from my meeting to find that it had begun to snow. *Snow.* Whatever you south-of-the-forty-ninth-parallel people might think, we in southeastern Ontario do not "do" snow until at least mid-November, and we don't normally have snowplow-level snow for at least a couple of weeks after that—sometimes not until the beginning of the new year. Yet, in this first week of November, we were getting appreciable amounts of the white stuff, and it was sticking around long enough to bring out the unmistakable crashing rumble of the snowplows.

But there were no snowplows outside this evening, and my snow tires were still in the garage. I had a forty-minute drive by highway from the city to home, and it was full dark.

I hate driving in snow at night. Night driving, sure; driving in snow, no problem (hey, I'm Canadian!). It's the combination that makes me antsy. For one thing, visibility is terrible. There's that strange visual sensation you get of being attacked by a gazillion tiny white projectiles; the flakes come at you in your headlights' glare as though they were aliens swarming your car. However rational you are, if you aren't used to this it's pretty spooky. Worse still, without a visible landscape to tether yourself to, it's easy to get badly disoriented—a sort of nocturnal white-out. You can't see lane markings, which is bad enough, but because it's night you also can't see the roadside, which greatly increases your fear of driving right off the road and into a ditch. Because this is swampy country, some of our ditches are formidable.

No, I don't drive at night in snow. Not if I can help it.

Tonight I couldn't help it.

By the time I got onto the four-lane highway southbound, the road was gray and greasy with snow and slush, and it got steadily worse. I hoped to find a convoy of vehicles to join; that way, you follow the leader's tail lights instead of constantly having to search the landscape for clues as to where the road is or isn't. But there was no convoy.

No; correction. There was a convoy. It was forming up with me in the lead.

Expletive deleted.

It was coming down harder and faster and I couldn't see the road at all; I had to rely on the rumble strips at the side of the road to tell me if I was about to drive off onto the shoulder. I slowed up, hoping someone would pass. Fat chance. The cars behind me slowed obediently. Nobody likes being lead car in night snow like this.

So, with me in the lead, about twenty-five cars crept south at about two-thirds of the speed limit. I refused to think about such auxiliary terrors as black ice and dumb road-crossing critters, although it did occur to me to thank God that we were too far south for moose. I counted the landmarks: Bankfield Road, Mud Creek, Stevens Creek, Roger Stevens Drive, Cranberry Creek, Dilworth Road. Ah, thank God, the bridge over the river, the bridge that means I'm almost to my exit. River Road.

Then the big truck boomed up on my left, just as the River Road on-ramp merged to my right. The big guys don't mind these conditions at all; they're used to driving in weather like this. They don't mean to be unkind to the rest of us poor benighted cowards, but they have schedules to keep and a living to make and there's no way they're going to reduce speed to join a convoy. They cut through the crud and keep going.

He was going the speed limit or better. As he passed his tires kicked up a blinding snow swirl and then he cut back in, much too close, his rear wheels throwing up veils of snow so thick that I couldn't even see his tail lights as he raced off into the night. With the extra on-ramp lanes to my right, I had no idea whatsoever where the edge of the road was. I couldn't pull over and stop because of the cars following too close behind me; to slow up was to risk a major skid and a pile-up. I was lost and helplessly in motion, and I was scared out of my living gourd.

I don't know why it hadn't occurred to me, until that very moment, that maybe prayer might be a good idea. I'm usually unnecessarily slow on the uptake with this one. Partly it's because I have spent irritated time with people who had to pray over every hammer stroke as they set a nail, but mostly it's because I tend to be an independent cuss. "OK, God, I can handle this, no reason to bother You"—as though somehow God *minds* being prayed to, or there's a seriousness quotient that a situation has to meet for prayer to be allowable, or there's some limit on the number of times that I'm allowed to ask, some magical quota that I can't afford to use up for trivial things such as being helpless and terrified. My head usually knows better, but my head is not the part of me in charge of prayer. My soul usually feels it's safer not to depend on anyone else; that way, you won't use up their good will or invite rejection or indifference.

But now, caught in this nightmare snow dance, prayer was clearly required. I couldn't summon the self-collection to put together prayer-type words, just a general inner cry: *Be with me, please. Get me home safely.*

I can't say that the wind died down and the snow cleared and the moon came out. In fact, the wind picked up, making the snow swirl even harder and sending my small car shuddering as though the tires were slipping on the slick pavement. But we were held straight somehow, the car and I, blinded as I still was. It was still guesswork, staying on the road as the convoy snaked behind me.

I suppose a psychologist would say that by praying I had reduced my own anxiety level enough to function more efficiently.

Maybe so, maybe not. I was aware of an inner quietness that silenced the yammer of anxiety; perhaps it was a sort of spiritual placebo. I didn't really know, or care. I did my road finding in a state of semi-autopilot without being particularly conscious of what I was doing. Consciousness no longer came into it. I'm sure of that.

I was still in this oddly peaceful state when, carefully tracking the right edge of the road as best I could, I found myself heading slightly uphill as a green exit sign loomed up suddenly on my right: Leeds and Grenville County Road 43. I hadn't found my exit; it found me. Thanks be to God. Several cars followed me. I wondered briefly whether they really meant to get off at this exit or were still blindly following my taillights.

Did prayer get me home? I don't believe in magical thinking. I've seen how prayer can become that, and how destructive magical-thinking theology can be. So no, I don't think I got home safely because God intervened and took over the driving. But I do think that sometimes when things go right, something in me aligns with God's love, and somehow the two of them carry me out of danger into safety, out of hurt into healing, out of hell into life. It's happened fairly regularly, enough that I should trust the process more than I remember to do.

Turning at the stoplight into town, my car did her first major skid of the winter, and I corrected smoothly, automatically, without thinking. Ah, winter. Home again.

ৰ Psalm 91 ৰ

He who dwells in the shelter of the Most High
abides under the shadow of the Almighty.
He shall say to the Lord,

"You are my refuge and my stronghold,
my God in whom I put my trust."

I remember, in childhood, looking through a book of photographs of World War II, and finding in it pictures of what looked like stacked brushwood—until my six-year-old eyes looked more closely and saw that they were bodies, naked and emaciated. For whatever reason, I had not one moment's denial of what I'd seen, of the reality of it, its truthfulness, its horror. For years, whenever I heard this psalm I thought of these people, these Jews of Europe, praying it, whispering it to themselves and their children:

He shall deliver you from the snare of the hunter,
and from the deadly pestilence.
He shall cover you with his pinions,
and you shall find refuge under his wings;
his faithfulness shall be a shield and buckler.

"Curse God and die," Job's wife tells him. Curse him because he's made all these promises; he's said that if you're good and follow the rules, he will favor you and everything will be all right. But look at where you are. Either you've broken some rule—maybe a rule you don't even know about—or God has reneged on the deal. But one way or another, the trust is broken. How can you have faith in a God who promises so much good and apparently delivers so much hurt?

You shall not be afraid of any terror by night,
nor of the arrow that flies by day;
of the plague that stalks in the darkness,
nor of the sickness that lays waste at midday.

Later, when I was older, I got fascinated by history, especially the history of the English Middle Ages, and smack-dab in the middle of that history there is the Black Death. The people facing this inexplicable disaster, priests and people, nobility and peasantry, would have prayed this psalm in desperation, trying hard to believe it, as a third of the population sickened horribly and died.

For he shall give his angels charge over you,
to keep you in all your ways.
They shall bear you in their hands,
lest you dash your foot against a stone.

Right. Sure.

Of course, a person couldn't live through the latter half of the twentieth century without encountering other horrors: Northern Ireland, Cambodia, Ethiopia, Somalia, Bosnia, Rwanda, the Congo, Afghanistan, the Middle East, the Sudan . . . times when human evil apparently won out over whatever goodness God seems able to exert in this terrible, hurting world, times when no angels came to bear up the innocent. No divine catcher's mitt appeared in the heavens to field the airplanes on 9/11. No obvious angels were in action at Middle School 1 in Beslan, handing out water and comforting the terrified children or tackling the hostage takers. No seraphim stood between the people of South Asia and the tsunami.

You shall tread upon the lion and adder;
you shall trample the young lion and the serpent
under your feet.

Sometimes it seems that this world is almost too horrible to live in, although that sentiment probably has quite a lot to do with the selective attention of the news media. I have to remember that I live in a country where public massacres don't happen, where we are (mostly) peaceful and prosperous; I am extremely fortunate in that regard. I have never had to face such horrors, except through the filter of newspapers and TV.

But not all bad times are the obvious, dramatic ones; for most of us the lions and adders are quieter ones, more personal, more domestic. I have stubbed my toes on more than a few rocks and I hit them again recently against another one, a big one.

So there I was, sitting in church—not in the choir stalls with my choral chums, but in a front pew off to the side, where I could struggle through the service, singing when I could and shutting up when I couldn't, honking into my handkerchief obbligato. Once again, my toes were bloodied by those damned stones. This time it was a very large stone—the end of a hopeful marriage—and my toes were really hurting. No angels came and bore me up, not this time. Mind you, this has not in general been my experience of the way things work. These toes have encountered any number of stones. They are scarred with the bites of lion cubs and the burn marks of dragonlets. They *hurt*.

We were saying Psalm 91 together. Or rather, the reader and congregation were saying it together. I was listening mostly, because my voice was so badly choked by tears.

And yet, and yet. It was different, this time. This time, I was not alone with this suffering; I was surrounded by a cloud of concern. Much of it came from the choir stalls; they knew what I was going through and why I had to be here in the pew instead of with them. Don, the priest, a big golden bear, glanced at me from time to time; when I ran into him before the service, he surrounded me with a huge hug. If I needed hands-on love, I needed only to go up to the altar rail after the service and the hands of kindness would be there, and the prayers.

Now, for the first time, I was not in flat-out rebellion against this psalm; I was not yelling in my head to God "You liar! You *promised!"* I was swimming with, not against, the psalm, and it was bearing me up. This time, it felt true in a weird, paradoxical way.

It gets back to the nature of truth. The psalm isn't literally true. If it were literally true, God would have whipped down and snatched God's chosen people out of the hands of their persecutors, instead of enduring with them as they suffered. If it were literally true, Rwanda's churches wouldn't have been full of corpses and the children of Beslan and Aceh Province would be happily at play. It doesn't matter what we think God should have done under the circumstances; either we don't believe in God at all, or we understand that God doesn't operate as we think God should.

But there is a deeper truth, and I felt it working its way up from my poor bloodied toes as we moved through the psalm:

> *Because he is bound to me in love,*
> *therefore will I deliver him;*
> *I will protect him, because he knows my name.*

It's not that these things don't happen—the stubbed toes, the lions and adders, and the plagues by night and the sicknesses laying waste at noontime. It's that with God's grace and the love of our fellow pilgrims—our angels who bear us up—we have the ability to make something out of suffering. We have the power to redeem it and give it meaning, and therefore to triumph over it. Being bound to God in love gives me the possibility.

I find there's a rhythm in the psalms, one of those deep-truth rhythms: the yells of complaint and fearfulness and terrible pain are followed by songs of the sweetest, most peaceful trust. I think of the psalms of the deepest faith: Psalm 23, of course, but also Psalm 131, the one about sitting peacefully on God's lap like a toddler. What comes before each of them? A cry in the dark.

For me, at least, it never seems to be "Save me *from* the time of trial" but "save me *in* the time of trial." The trials seem just to be part of the landscape, because I am an ordinary, moderately screwed-up person who sometimes makes lousy choices. The miracle is that God does bring me through and out the other side.

So I found the psalm's deeper truth: in the fullness of eternity I will be able to look back and see that God has been my refuge and my stronghold, my God in whom I put my trust, and that God's protection has been with me through all fields of stones, in all the times of plague, in facing lions and adders.

> *She shall call upon me, and I will answer her;*
> *I am with her in trouble;*
> *I will rescue her and bring her to honor.*
> *With long life will I satisfy her,*
> *and show her my salvation.* *

There; the psalm was finished, and I had done with my crying, at least for now. I found my place in the hymnal and rose, refreshed.

ᕀ The Light on the Water ᕀ

What drew me down to the water's edge was the light. There was enough of a southwesterly wind to give the lake a bit of a ruffle, and the sun, even partly veiled by cloud wisps, was lighting the water in a broad strip of dappled brilliance, leading the eye out into broader, deeper waters. So I found a spot for my car and walked down past the limestone houses, around the bridge and past where the ducks hang out, along by the old pier, to the tiny shingle beach, braving the wind, which was whippy and not quite cold.

*Unlike other quotations from the Psalms in this book, which use the New Revised Standard Version, the quotations from Psalm 91 use the version found in *The Book of Alternative Services of the Anglican Church of Canada.*

The light moved as I did, naturally. You pursue light on water, but you don't actually ever catch it; children learn that one very early. But at the shingle beach, the light seemed to stop, and so did I. I looked out at it, the glow of the water against the softness of sky.

It came back to me then, a certainty that I'd lost for a while, one that I thought I might have lost for good, in fact: the certainty of God's ultimate victory over all the forces that divide us from love. I'd gotten sadly cynical about love of late; I'd seen it bash itself like this water against the rocks, making no apparent difference, retreating in what looked like defeat, into the silence of a death. I'd seen how spirituality can become a way of evading one's own real issues, how supposedly "turning toward God" can actually be a full-out flight from painful realities. I'd retreated myself into the silence, not of unbelief or disbelief, but of belief suspended in chaos and pain. I had found myself retreating into a silence devoid of any whisper of God.

Yet here was the light on the water, no longer moving, still not reachable, but *there*. Just for a moment, I knew that, however little it looked this way to me, I too was standing in the same light. I knew, however briefly, that even though I felt like a darkness absorbing the light, to God I was water reflecting it in glory. The wind died down for a moment, and just for the moment I felt all the warmth of the April sun.

I thought how quiet God's victories might be. Maybe for some, there's the glorious knock-you-off-your-donkey experience, but that's never been my way; always for me, it's not the rainbow but the groundwater quietly seeping up from sources I can't begin to imagine. I thought of the quiet sense of right that comes in the stillness left by the clamor and shrillness of wrong; of the painful, healing silence that enters when the shouting falters, exhausted; of the emptying out that leaves you not lonely but peaceably alone.

After the riotous crowds, first adoring, then hostile, after the screams and the suffering, there's the quiet of the tomb, and it looks at first like utter defeat. But then, in the deepest stillness that comes before the first birds wake, there's the soundless rise and fall of the chest, the whoosh of blood, the whispered singing of synapses. Only the smallest sounds as the shroud comes off and he sits up, swinging around, setting his feet noiselessly on the cool stone that neither cries nor shatters but silently takes his weight.

This past Easter I fasted from joy, turning my back on proclamations, alleluias, trumpets, and the loud singing of joyful hymns; instead, I feasted on silence, the quiet and steady lap of ruffled water, the silence of this light, the only sound that of the wind. There's where I could sense the real victory, the one that endures: love *will* have its way in the end, and "all will be well and all will be well and all manner of things will be well." Maybe not today or tomorrow, maybe not even next year. But inevitably, when God and I are ready.

CHAPTER 5

Saints Ancient and Modern

Come, bless the Lord, all you servants
of the Lord,
who stand by night in the house
of the Lord!
Lift up your hands to the holy place,
and bless the Lord.
May the Lord, maker of heaven
and earth,
bless you from Zion.

—PSALM 134

❧ White China ❧

A few days before Christmas, my younger kid got down our creche set, unwrapped all the figures, and set them up on top of the china cabinet, next to the Christmas tree. The set was given to me some years ago by a friend. It's plain white china, very pure and tasteful. It has the manger with the Christ Child in it, the figures of Mary and Joseph, a couple of shepherds, the three Wise Men, camels, an ox, two donkeys, a trio of sheep, and an angel. The set will stay out until Epiphany, when I'll wrap all the figures up again and put them away in their box until next Christmas.

That's a pretty normal mainline Christian approach to Mary. We take this pure, featureless, colorless figurine out at Christmas; we put her back in her box again at Epiphany. We don't go for gaudy overdecorated Mary figures in crowns, or bleeding hearts, or stuff like that; we've rejected the older, more flowery Blessed Virgin Mary traditions of Roman Catholicism, and we really don't know much of anything about the mystical traditions of Eastern Orthodoxy, or for that matter about more modern Roman Catholic approaches. We Anglicans are apt to have a discreet, featureless sort of Mary, one we don't think very much about, except at this time of year.

Who was this young woman? We know very little about her, really, just a few references in the Gospels, many of them strangely uncomfortable. There's actually more about Mary in the Islamic Qur'an than there is in the Christian New Testament. The only other sources of "information" are a number of scriptures that weren't included in the canonical New Testament, documents like the apocryphal Gospel of James, which says that Mary was the daughter of Joachim and Anna and was miraculously conceived.

A great deal of traditional doctrine about Mary is actually more poetry than anything else; this is where the beliefs about her perpetual virginity come from. Or doctrine arises from what people thought *should* be true—for example, that God must have planned this all from the beginning of the universe, foreordaining Mary's acceptance from the very start. Or doctrine comes out of early church debates on the nature of Christ, the source of the Orthodox doctrine about Mary the God bearer (Theotokos).

All we really know from the Gospels is that Mary was a young Jewish woman, probably only a girl in her teens, betrothed to Joseph but not yet living with him in any sense of the word, when the angel came to tell her she would bear God's son. We know that Mary and Joseph were both observant Jews; we know this from their presentation of Jesus in the Temple. She seems to have been a thoughtful person; we're told she took things to heart and pondered them.

We know, from the story of the marriage of Cana, that she was proud of her remarkable son and wanted to show him off. We know that sometimes they struggled; it's not clear whether Mary really understood what Jesus was about, at least at first. We are fairly sure that she watched her son die on the Cross, surely the worst pain a person can go through, and that he commended her to the protection of his beloved disciple. We know she was with the disciples in Jerusalem after Christ's ascension. This is roughly all the Gospel information we have about Mary.

But if you think about it, some other things start to emerge. Look at the Gospel of the Annunciation. The angel comes to Mary and says, "Mary, God thinks so highly of you that he has chosen you to bear his son." Mary says yes to God. She does question *how* she can do this, since she's still a virgin, but that's her only hesitation.

She doesn't say, "'Scuse me, do you mind waiting a minute while I check this with my intended?" She simply says, "Yes, I'll do it, God."

Now, her yes has been interpreted as total obedience, a sort of passive acceptance of her fate, something she didn't have any real choice about. That's where we get Mary as the ultimate pre-programmed Goody Two-Shoes. This image of absolute obedience has had terrible consequences for women through the ages. Women were measured against the image and found always wrong and lacking—Eve's daughters, not Mary's sisters. "Alone of all her sex she pleased the Lord," the Roman poet Caelius Sedulius wrote: well, what does that say about all the rest of us? Mary was a standard none of the rest of womankind could ever live up to.

But what if her yes was a free choice? What if she had the choice to say no? After all, God was asking her to take some very, very big risks. She had no way of knowing that Joseph wouldn't cast her off. After all, he would be the one person who knew for absolutely certain that Jesus wasn't his child. He might not believe her; he might be hurt and furious. Maybe she had that much trust in Joseph's love, but in fact, the Gospel of Matthew says he did come close to repudiating her. That would mean total ruin for her, expulsion from her family and community and perhaps even death by stoning. She would be without a home or any support, totally disgraced. Even today, women in the Middle East who are thought to have had illicit sex are routinely murdered for the honor of their families.

So what God was asking of her was a big deal indeed. Yet she said yes, immediately.

I prefer to think that Mary said yes not out of blind, passive obedience but out of radical faith: "Yes, Lord, this is a really big thing you're asking of me, and I can't see how it's going to turn out, but I'll trust you completely on it." I don't see her being mild as milk; I see her with her head thrown back in triumphant acceptance. The gospeler Luke, remembering Hannah's song over the conception of her son Samuel, gives Mary a mighty song to sing.

My soul magnifies the Lord,
and my spirit rejoices in God my Savior,
for he has looked with favor on the lowliness of his servant.
Surely, from now on all generations will call me blessed;
for the Mighty One has done great things for me, and holy is
* his name.*
His mercy is for those who fear him from generation to
* generation.*
He has shown strength with his arm;
he has scattered the proud in the thoughts of their hearts.
He has brought down the powerful from their thrones,
and lifted up the lowly;
he has filled the hungry with good things
and sent the rich away empty.
He has helped his servant Israel, in remembrance of his
* mercy,*
according to the promise he made to our ancestors,
to Abraham and to his descendants forever.
—LUKE 1:46B-55

It's not a namby-pamby, pure-white china song. It's full of triumph and challenge, the joyous chant of a young revolutionary; this is a God who's going to turn everything inside-out and upside-down, a God who's going to tumble the rich and powerful out of their seats, a God who's going to upend the social order. Maidenly modesty doesn't come anywhere near it. This isn't a simpering young lady, with downcast eyes and narrow white hands pressed together in pious prayer and with golden waving hair flowing down her back. This is a strong-minded young Jewish woman with black hair and flashing dark eyes and red cheeks: think of young

Palestinian or Israeli women today in their vivid, substantial beauty. She's not dressed in pastels; she's wearing homespun, dyed with whatever plants were available. Her feet are bare and callused. She is courageous, faithful, intelligent, and deeply loving, because God would choose nothing less to be the mother of his Son. But a sweet demure young thing? I don't think so.

Is she "gentle Mary, meek and mild"? Maybe, although I'd like to think her Son got his considerable temper from his mama. "Meek and mild" sounds a bit too much like a man's idea of what a nice girl should be like. What she must have been is strong, strong enough to take on the job in the first place, strong enough to face down her husband and family when she told them, strong enough to face exile, strong enough to survive the Crucifixion. Whatever Mary was, she wasn't a weakling.

Set aside the conventional images. Don't think of Mary kneeling upright before the manger, worshiping her Savior. No woman who's just given birth is going to do that. Think of her lying back in the straw, her hair loose and her forehead sweaty after the bloody, violent business of birth, this girl, cradling her newborn baby, who probably looked like a monkey—most newborns do. She's holding him in the crook of her arm, touching his tiny hands and face. The two of them are figuring out how to nurse. It takes some practice. She's exhausted and happy and triumphant, and Joseph close by her, loving the two of them, is exhausted and happy too.

Why does this matter so much? Because Mary and Joseph, those two good Jews, are also the first to follow Christ. They are our oldest siblings, the first of the great company of pilgrims. Their humanity matters. God comes to us not when we're perfect white china figures, but in all our messy, meaty humanity, our confusion and pain. God didn't choose Mary because she was a characterless doll; he chose her for her courage, her boldness, her capacity for vibrant love. He loves us *for* our humanity, not in spite of it.

As these very human people could welcome Christ into their lives, so can we. Mary accepts Jesus literally into her body, carries him inside her for those months while his own body forms and grows, and then she bears him in all the pain and glorious squalor of childbirth. We take the Holy Spirit into our own selves, and we are as radically transformed by it as Mary's body was transformed by pregnancy. It's not an abstract image; it's what incarnation is all about. *Carne,* the very soul of the word *incarnation,* means "flesh" or "meat." This is not an abstract, bloodless sort of business. God meets us exactly where we are, here, now, in our own bodies, in our own lives.

I know it's much easier to picture the Nativity scene in white china, because painting a realistic scene is so much more difficult. We can be so afraid of making Mary too garish that we don't give her any color at all. But God seems to love this world just as it is, in all its messy immediacy. That's why he chose to dwell among us, after all. He loved Mary all the more for her being a vivid, strong figure instead of a passive, sweet young thing.

I have to say, as one strong-minded woman to another, that I think I like her better this way. If the only women God wants are the gentle, meek, and mild ones, I'm in deep trouble, for certain. I need this big sister of mine, this brave and faithful young woman, Mary. She can teach me honesty, love, and courage. She deserves my honor, respect, and dear affection.

❧ Dreamer ❧

After Epiphany, it's time to put the creche set away for another year. I get a small, sturdy cardboard box and a supply of big, soft paper napkins and begin to wrap the pieces up, starting with the largest (camels) and working my way down to the smallest (Christ Child in manger). Midway through the process I stop for a moment, regarding the small straight-backed male figure in my hand.

We know so little about Joseph, really. We have two contradictory genealogies linking him to David, and everyone who reads them no doubt thinks, "And just why does this matter, since he wasn't Jesus' father anyway?" We know that he was a "just" or "righteous" man who, even without angelic intervention, would have treated Mary as decently as he could. We know other snippets: he and Mary went every year from Nazareth to the Temple in Jerusalem; he worked as a carpenter. Matthew implies he came from Judea; Luke suggests he came from Nazareth. But that's really about it. Everything else in our traditions comes from the apocryphal Gospel of James or from early legends.

Those of us who don't belong to the Roman Catholic or Orthodox tradition spend even less time with Joseph than we do with Mary. We're not sure what to *do* with him. This is partly because he's so tied in with the vexed and slightly squeamish subject of Mary's virginity (please, people, can we see these two as something other than sexual non-partners?). It's also partly that we have so little to work with, and what there is we don't have the courage to use imaginatively.

With some exceptions. Martin Smith makes one important deduction: we know from the way that Jesus talks about God as *Abba,* Daddy, that Jesus knew the feel of true paternal love. Joseph plays a crucial role in that respect. This alone would make him an extraordinary man. Even now, some men (and probably some women too) have trouble accepting a child who's not their own; they resent the kid as an intruder, an unwelcome reminder of Mom's previous relationship. To a man of Joseph's culture and period, accepting a child who was not his—and Joseph would have *known* that—is almost unimaginable. Nonetheless, Smith imagines Joseph bending down to scoop up this little kid who is not his in the flesh but who is *his* in the heart, swooping the child up over his head, as daddies do, the two of them laughing together in love. Jesus is extraordinarily tender with children, and protective. Where did he learn how to father but from this heart-father?

I love this image of Joseph in all its freshness and color, this vibrant lover of Mary and father of a fine family. But another thing emerges from the Gospel, the one that interests me the most: this business of dreaming. Joseph, for a practical man, seems to have been a mighty dreamer, like his Old Testament namesake. This is what the Joseph texts are about, and this is how he gets all his instructions: angels appear to him in dreams and tell him what to do next. *Yes, it's OK, accept Mary and her child; name the child Jesus.* And *Watch out! Herod's after the baby's life; get yourselves to a place of safety.* And *It's OK, you can go home now.*

I've had spiritual dreams too, although not often. They have a very different feeling to them from ordinary dreams. They are (I find) profoundly memorable in ways that other dreams are not. One, in particular, was so vivid and strong that I can still revisit it in memory more clearly than I can remember most days—and yes, it contained a depth of truth. Was this what Joseph experienced?

Are dreams like this simply a variant on other dreams—that is, was my unconscious tossing up something from the depths that it knew needed to be dealt with? Were the "angels" in Joseph's dreams actually his own intuition, clothing itself in angelic garb because this is how a religious mind works? Or should I take Joseph's position, that there are times when sleep becomes a sort of thin place where my soul meets the divine in a particular closeness, permitting a visionary sort of communication? The latter sounds so New-Agey that it makes me nervous. But maybe that's really what's happening.

Perhaps there's a wisdom that comes more freely when the walls of consciousness are down, when we aren't busy or preoccupied and God can come to us with a freedom that we might, if we were awake, resist—not intentionally, necessarily, but because we have our preconceptions and we're often not even aware of what they are. Maybe God can stir up images from our subconscious minds that are particularly spiritually communicative. Maybe Jung and the New Testament are closer together than we think.

I remember with precise and vivid detail a dream in which I left a gorgeous, splendid service in a great basilica and, passing through dreary corridors, found myself in a cool, dim, dusty room full of old furniture shrouded in dust covers. I curled up in the corner of a sofa and cried a little, for I was very tired, and then I slept; when I woke, a man was standing next to me—a lean, plain figure, nothing distinguished about him. He wore work clothes, clean and serviceable, but drab, and I knew at once that he had spent years among the poor. He took my hand and examined it and said with a great and courteous gentleness, "I see by your hand that you have been in exile." That's all he said, but I knew who he was, and I heard his unspoken promise that the exile would not be endless. I knew I could trust that promise.

We talk about following our dreams, though too often it means "I won't rest until I get what I want." Sometimes sheer determination can make our dreams come true. But sometimes our dreams lie outside our grasp. All dreams but one: the dream of salvation. This one begs to be grasped, held, and pursued with joy, and it can be relied upon completely—as completely as Joseph trusted what the Lord said to him in sleep.

A good man, that one, and one who deserves to be remembered in praise.

❧ Mary and Martha ❧

It is typical for women of my age and domestic persuasion to cast a certain jaundiced eye over Luke 10:38–42:

Now as they went on their way, he entered a certain village, where a woman named Martha welcomed him into her home. She had a sister named Mary, who sat at the Lord's feet and listened to what he was saying. But Martha was distracted by her many tasks; so she came to him and asked, "Lord, do you not care that my sister has left me to do all the work by myself? Tell her then to help me." But the Lord answered her, "Martha, Martha, you are worried and distracted by many things; there is need of only one thing. Mary has chosen the better part, which will not be taken away from her."

Huh, women my age think. Huh.

First of all, we don't see any of the men giving a hand—OK, that's normal for that time and culture, but still. Second, from experience we tend to believe that if we don't do the needful, the needful won't get done. Third, some of us at least understand that domesticity has its spiritual aspects, not all of them bad by any means, so it seems a little inappropriate for Jesus to call Mary's choice "the better part." If we all chose "the better part" all the time, how on earth would the laundry ever get done?

Martha and Mary are held up time and time again as opposites: works versus faith, action versus contemplation, doing versus being. Some have seen the story as giving out rank: faith is better than works, contemplation than action, being than doing.

But as always, context matters. This story comes immediately after the Parable of the Good Samaritan, which (as my Bible commentary points out) is its exact opposite. The Parable of the Good Samaritan is about men, and it's about giving care—about doing versus being, about works compared to faith, about action compared to contemplation. In the Samaritan story, the traditional role of the Jewish men in question (both of them Temple people) is to do the prayer-type stuff and leave the practicalities to some-one else, most especially the practicality of dealing with a bloodied and potentially dead body, which would pollute them and disable them for their traditional duties. Jesus issues a pretty strong rebuke to *that* notion.

It's this either-or business that causes the trouble, along with all the unexamined assumptions that Jesus insists on confronting, especially the ones about love. When we divide roles so that women have to carry the entire domestic burden, as they still do in much of the world, then we give Martha no time or freedom just to sit and think—unless she can sit and think while her spin-dle is twirling, instead of trying to plan the rest of the day so that the overwhelming volume of work gets done. When, because they're busy with professional stuff, we absolve men from the busi-ness of giving care as well as receiving it—as is still, sadly, far too common—then we don't include them in the full circle of human-ity. By letting them off the hook, we diminish and infantilize them. Yes, we can flip the genders so that she's a top executive and he's a house husband. Doesn't matter. What matters is that the inequality in caregiving leads to an imbalance for each, and a resulting failure to grow into the fullness of humanity.

When we set up works versus faith or doing versus being, we miss the need for *balance*. It has to do with integration, with bring-ing together the opposing needs and forces in one's own personal-ity instead of separating them off into opposing compartments. A lot of women have a need to give care, and there's nothing wrong with that, except they also need to learn to ask for care, which is where Martha is in the story. I don't think she's really so jealous of Mary's sitting out the domestic stuff; I think she's jealous of the fact that Mary is expressing her own need to sit down and be loved as well as loving. It's what Martha needs too, but she's too condi-tioned to being the lady of the household (which is what her name actually means) and to doing all the looking after. To go on giving and giving without expressing your own need for care, and having it listened to and accepted by those around you—that is to court a case of really poisonous self-pitying resentment, not to mention psychospiritual burnout. Jesus sees this in her. It says something important that instead of saying "Woman," as he does to so many other women—his own mother included—he calls to this busy, bustling friend of his quite gently, maybe even with his hand outreached and a smile in his voice, naming her in love: "Martha, Martha."

Likewise, in the preceding Good Samaritan passage, there's no point talking about how loving we are if we don't actually *do* something with it. The loving feeling can be just a way of making us feel good about ourselves. Love is active, not passive; it demands to have something to do. Love says it's not enough just to feel loving, because it can turn rapidly into a sort of warm bath of emotion that's all about thinking what nice people we are. "Nice people" is by no means the same as "good people"; indeed the two are sometimes inversely related. By choosing to value what nice people we are, we fail to face our own failings; but it's by facing and accepting the parts of ourselves we devalue that we find our way toward real goodness. The priest and Levite in the parable are perfectly nice guys. But the Samaritan is a good man.

Jesus is calling us into balance; he's looking at two instances in which the balance between being and doing is out of whack, and he is calling for a correction. He's challenging the assumptions—especially those about gender and roles—that keep us trapped in our imbalance. He's calling on us to leave off doing what we're best at, and to take on what we find uncomfortable. Martha may resent having to do all the serving, but it's the resentment of someone who's very good at what she does and expects recognition for it—a form of pride. For her, much as she thinks she desires to sit at Jesus' feet, it's going to be hard work *not* to jump up and see to the bread rising.

The two Jews in the Good Samaritan parable, if they'd acted in love, would have had to find their way into unfamiliar roles of humble caregiving. ("I can't tell what's wrong with him. Can you hold his head? Where do we find water? How do I tie off a bandage?"). Having to care for this beaten man would have left them uncertain about their abilities, and with blood on their best robes. It would have stretched them as people, which is not something that's comfortable but instead is very good for the soul.

So: all you good Marthas out there, put down that dishtowel and pull up a chair. Yes, it's hard. Do it. Make yourself sit there; rest and be thankful.

To all who have served less than you've been served, it's time *you* did the dishes.

Red Angels

I thought I had my face well under control—was taking minor pride, in fact, in doing such a fine job of stiff-upper-lipping it as I sat listening to the lessons. Having my face well under control was certainly what I most deeply wanted. I knew I was in no shape to sing in choir, this first week after my mother's funeral, so I found a spot off to the side in one of the front pews, out of everyone's line of sight as much as I could. Only the alto section could see me.

One of the hardest things about hard times is how we tend to isolate ourselves when we're in trouble. It's usually because that's what we've been taught to do. Think of family mottoes: "Don't air the dirty linen" and "Stiff upper lip!" and "Big girls don't cry" and "God helps those who help themselves." Aside from these ancient and not terribly helpful bromides, we may also have the painful experience of people not being there for us when we need them, sometimes because they don't want to be bothered but more often because either they weren't noticing or they didn't know what to do or say. Or because we didn't feel we could ask. Then, of course, there are those helpful souls who say things like, "You think you've got it tough? Let me tell you about *my* problems."

One way or another, it can be hard to admit that you really, really, *really* need a hug and a Kleenex. It's harder still when you don't know the people around you very well. Here I was, having just joined this parish a couple of months ago; I hadn't spent years washing dishes and listening to people and building up a store of liking and credibility to draw on when I needed help myself. Or that's how I generally tend to see it. How many of us really believe, down deep, that love is something we have to earn (often the hard way) and that our slight, frail hold on it can disappear with the slightest misstep?

(OK, you can all put your hands down now.)

So through the stresses of moving (dislocation, homesickness, being the new kid on the block) and the endlessness or fits-and-starts renovations (taking, naturally, six to eight weeks longer than anyone planned) and my mother's dying (with the inevitable upsurge of big, bad family issues), and a marriage coming miserably to pieces, and the standard stuff (book deadlines, emotional teenagers)—with all of this going on, I'd done my best to be civil, friendly, and smiley-faced in my new parish. In fact, when I really couldn't manage the smiley face, I thought it best to stay away. I hoped, I thought, I prayed that people wouldn't notice; they'd just assume I wasn't particularly churchy or something.

But this Sunday morning, however proud I was of my self-control, my face was clearly saying things behind my back. Someone in the choir noticed, for at the beginning of a hymn, two of the altos whispered a brief consultation and then rose as one and sailed briskly, red choir robes and white choir cottas billowing, through the chancel and down the steps to where I sat. Becky tucked her deft, small self in on my left and Mieke slipped in on my right, putting her arm around my shoulders. "You looked like you shouldn't be alone," Becky whispered.

I lost it.

When I was able to pay attention to the sermon, I heard Bob, our rector, talking about Mother Teresa—how, very late in her life, she told the College of Preachers "I am just a pencil in God's hand, writing love letters to the world."

Wow.

Bob then passed out pencils, the little stubby ones without erasers, telling us to take one, write someone a love letter, consider what it means to be a pencil in God's hand.

Well, yes, I do know something about making like a pencil, and I have written a few love letters; maybe I can even find new things to say. I pray that much. I tucked my pencil away in my PDA case so I wouldn't lose it.

Next to this—the real, practical practice of love, this being a pencil in God's hand—doctrinal exactitude isn't worth a tinker's dam. Next to this, church power politicking looks as childish as it really is. Next to this, the posturing of the righteously indignant and the needy-for-ego-strokes look not so much revolting as just plain pathetic. Next to this, mere warm fuzziness looks washed out and sounds boom-hollow. Next to this, my own sinfulness morphs into nothing much, while mystery dances and my soul blooms in all its fullest color. This is what it's about, folks.

There is no point talking about love unless we're prepared to *do* it. We can't assume that people know we love them, or that we're concerned about them, or that we want to help, not if we just sit in our pews whispering prayers for them but not making a move in their direction. They can't mind-read, after all.

We need to become communities in which people have the courage to go up to those in trouble and say, "What can I do to help?" It's hard, given our "chosen frozen" tradition, to snap through the conventions, the proprieties (and we know that the conventions and the proprieties are there for cause). It's also hard because we've all had the experience of being drawn into an emotional bottomless pit of one sort or another, having to give a whole lot more than we wanted to. But when fear—whether of saying the wrong thing, or making a fool of oneself, or risking a bottomless pit—stands in the way of our ministering to others, then we are failing to work out God's purpose. We are failing to be, for others, Christ with the warm human skin.

The same frustration of God's purpose happens when we're too proud (or more likely too scared) to ask for help. But that's where I'd been.

Eventually Becky had to go back up to choir; she's part of an instrumental group that had a gig at the offertory. A little later I told Mieke to go back too; we don't have enough altos to spare any at the communion hymns. But their comfort stayed with me right to the end of church, and beyond.

The choir doesn't march out at the end of the service in our parish; instead, after the dismissal, the choir comes down into the nave and everybody mingles to wish each other the peace of Christ. Becky and Mieke, my two red angels, sailed down again to hug me then, but so did my fellow tenor Dan and bass Jim, and I don't know how many others. I hugged them all and smiled and cried and told them that if this isn't a parish where people may cry in public, I will damn well see that it becomes one. We will become a parish in which there is a Kleenex box in every second pew. I'll buy the Kleenex. I promise.

(For the Rev. Bob Hales and the choir at St. James, Kingston, Ontario)

Matt

The day Matt died, I walked into walls for a while, and then I changed my guitar strings. I needed one of those unthinking yet demanding jobs, something that takes your complete concentration but doesn't require any real intellectual input. My mind wasn't truly with me; it was floating around, looking for Matt: "Just a flippin' minute, guy. You aren't supposed to leave yet. Not without saying goodbye."

I'd known him for a bit more than six years, without ever having actually met him. He was on the big Anglican e-mail list when I joined it, and out of that ebullient confusion his voice stood out, sometimes loud, often funny, frequently passionate, occasionally just plain over-the-edge impossible. He'd served in Vietnam and been a military chaplain. He was (it was obvious) an extremely good parish priest.

He was tough and thoughtful, high-spirited and opinionated (especially about barbecue, a matter of deep Texan passion and pride). He had a temper, which he not infrequently lost, and he could be wrong. But when he crossed the line he'd apologize like a gentleman, and when he was wrong he was more than big enough to admit it. He had a wart-hog side, and an ornery side, and he certainly knew it all. Yet there was always that sweetness to him, the sweetness of a really good apple, and a small-boy streak that seemed odd because he was so obviously one of the really truly grown-ups.

Above all, he had those qualities for which English is lacking words: *joie de vivre, esprit, panache.* He was *alive* as very few are ever really alive.

He couldn't be dead. It wasn't possible.

His death was all of a sudden. He went outside for a cigar while his wife went off to bed, and when she got up in the morning, there he was on the patio, dead. Since his death sneaked up on us, I hope it sneaked up on him too. I hope it didn't scare him too much. I hope he tumbled right into the palm of God's hand, considerably astonished and protesting that he had to get back to his family and his parish. When I heard of the suddenness of his death, I felt such stabs of grief and pity for those he left behind, who weren't granted the chance to say goodbye and who lacked the chance to kiss him as his soul slipped through their hands and into God's. Myself included.

It seems so strange that I can have known people face-to-face for years, and still have so much less true knowledge of the other than I can of people who I know only by electrons sculpted on very distant keyboards and sent through the ether via spiderwebs of hubs and fiber-optic lines. I *knew* Matt: knew the fresh, sound, sweet-saltiness of his soul. I had tasted his brotherly love for me, and found it true and healthy. I can remember coming down, one Sunday morning, and finding a casual post from him in my inbox, just a bit of affection and appreciation, and it was exactly like drinking a glass of cold fresh milk when you're hot and hungry and maybe a little bit scared. His sturdy affection supported my soul when it most needed support. He called my mother "not-my-mama," meaning that she was.

Some crying fits need Kleenex; some need paper towels; some need real big absorbent cotton hankies. Matt's death had me reaching for the big dinner napkins, the old soft cotton damask gone whiskery around the edges through long use and too much laundering. That bad.

Dammit, Matt, you weren't supposed to leave, not yet. Get back here! We weren't done with you yet. And my nose is sore.

Still, I had to do something, other than walk around the house banging into the woodwork. So I restrung the guitar, tuned it, and tuned it a couple more times (the inevitable result of restringing). I dug out the guitar arrangement I'd made of "Shall We Gather at the River," the one with all the interesting accidentals, not meant to be bounced through at Baptist-summer-camp high speed and major-key cheer, but to be sung slowly and with deep intention. I played it softly, to myself and Matt and to all the community of cyberspace in which we'd met and found ourselves loving and being beloved.

I remembered a time, a few years ago, when some of us in cyberspace imagined ourselves into a silly, special place called Humberside, with Land-of-Oz rules: our president was a grave and serious dean of law who was also a thirteen-year-old girl, and the silliness was particular and piercingly sweet. Matt was our fictional archbishop, as well as the (imaginary) Admiral of the Fleet of the Republic of Texas. It was a foolish time, and in time it passed, but it left something with us, who had been there: a vision of what, perhaps, lies ahead—of the deep foolishness of God, the playfulness of those who have suffered much and worked hard, the whooping silliness when we finally get whopped cross-eyed by the sheer love of God, the giddiness of grace.

I saw then a great silver river, calm, bright, deliciously coolwarm and full of delight and deep healing. Alongside it ran deep green banks, places to rest and be thankful, places where truly "we shall walk and worship ever / All the happy golden days." I saw there a community of love. I knew, really *knew,* that it was real, and that I would find it in God's good time.

We made true community then, and we have broken it and remade it over and over again. We have found that there is a truthfulness of soul that can wing its way from one computer to another, at a level of trust that is simply staggering. We have cried out to each other in the middle of the night, in pure desperation, and we have been caught and steadied and held in love. It can happen. It requires only that we take the Internet and point it Godward, which can be done. It's merely a matter of choosing which road to follow. Sadly, it's so often the road not taken.

I think of the picnic by the River when I think of Matt, and I think of his running the River-side barbecue *his* way, because he was a Texan and Texans know there's only one way to do barbecue, and that's the Texan way. I imagine much razzing about barbecue in heaven. I used to tease him by calling his beloved state Baja Oklahoma. He used to tease me about being Canadian; maybe my country was bigger'n his, but only till it thawed.

But that time did show me what Heaven might be like: a place of such unimaginable delight, such blessed companionship, such sheer pleasure; a Heaven far more interesting than any pallid matter of clouds and angels, a Heaven full of sharply and delight-fully individuated people. He's there now, or getting ready; and I am *so* @#$%! jealous.

When each of us crosses the River, there will be Matt, the Muttster, whooping like a true Texan and scrambling through the shallows to grab us, bear-hug us, slap our butts, and swing us up onto that blessed shore. That would be such a Matt thing to do.

Matt, I do love you, and I will miss you more than I can say. May those who mourn you, especially your best-beloved wife and kids, find comfort and support in the days to come. My brother, dearly beloved, go in peace, to love and serve the Lord.

But damn, I'd love to have you back. We weren't done yet. Not nearly.

ఈ Hymns ఈ

All right, all right, I confess it: my lower lip is out, right into the next county. At choir rehearsal I learned that (1) in spite of the fact that Sunday is All Saints Day, we will *not* be singing "For All the

Saints," and (2) we will be singing a hymn I particularly detest, "They Will Know We Are Christians by Our Love." (Yes, I know: it's a hymn much beloved by others, but not by me.) "For All the Saints" just happens to be my very favorite hymn (with "Deck Thyself, My Soul, with Gladness" a close second). I love the magnificent rumbly walking bass part and the splendid fistfuls of chords. I love the words. I adore the tune. Belting out "Alleluia!" with every muscle in my body is my idea of bliss. I rejoice in the tenor part in verses 4, 5, 6. "The golden evening brightens in the west" brings tears to my eyes, without fail, and gives me the deepest hope.

"They Will Know We Are Christians," on the other hand, drives me a little batty. It's all about unity, love, and everybody being at one—in theory exactly what God wants, but in practice? Let's get real here. Christians have been unloving each other, disputing each other, forming micro-churches fueled by self-righteousness and (often) rage and self-pity, shunning each other as cootie-ridden sinners, from the very get-go. There has not, so far as I know, been one decade of real Christian peace. People talk about "tradition"; well, that's the tradition: that I'm right and you're wrong, and (in the old days) the wrong guy will fetch up burning in agony foreverandeveramen, and boy, does that make the righteous jubilant.

What is it about religion that brings out the human nature in humans with such stunning regularity? I can feel it happening to myself: I can feel my desire for being right pushing me (sometimes) into arrogance or self-righteousness. It's really hard to be humble when you *know* you've got Truth in a half-nelson. It's really hard to love somebody who not only disagrees with you about something you feel is really important, but doesn't back down in the face of your (unimpeachable) arguments. It's this that Jesus recognized when he talked about the cost of the Kingdom, how it would bring strife and divisions. He wasn't prescribing "this is the way it should be"; he was predicting "this is what's going to happen," just as he predicted the Crucifixion. (An important distinction, prediction versus prescription.)

Why does it have to be like this? Partly, it's because to the faithful faith matters so very much. Partly it's because God, for God's good reasons, does not "do" skywriting; we have to interpret the truths we have received for our own times and our own circumstances, as both the theologians and the historians correctly tell us. God expects me to use my loaf, and my loaf may come up with different answers than yours does. Partly it's because so much of what we have received is mystery, apparently contradictory truths that we have to hold together, and this is hard work—easier to put down in black and white what is truly in shape-shifting radiant color. We want the either-or, not the both-and, but either-or just doesn't work particularly well. Partly it's because our understanding of this Creation is still unfolding and incomplete.

Partly it's just us. Look around the embattled landscape and what you see is a fusion of Christianity with other things: cultural assumptions about what's good (winning) and what's bad (losing); cultural preoccupations amounting to obsession (sex) regardless of what Scripture says is important (inequality and oppression); personal agendas, usually unspoken, often unrecognized. We put such a high value on being right that we fail to take into account the deep necessity of being wrong, to prune our self-righteousness back to a healthy level. The good Lord alone knows what undealt-with emotional and psychological issues we project on Those Evil Awful People Over There. Faced with our own deep sense of wrongness, our need to see ourselves as right and lovable, it's emotionally far cheaper and easier to battle the opposition than it is to struggle with our own need for healing. Hey, I do this too.

"They'll know that we're Christians by our love"; I don't think so. Not on the basis of our behavior. They'll know we are Christians by our squabbling, by our refusal to listen, really *listen*; by the joy we take in seeing the splinter in the other guy's eye; by our naysaying; by our judgmental attitude; by our nitpicking and legalism; by our pessimism; and by our refusal to accept that sometimes different isn't wrong, it's just different. I wish I could say that they'll know we are Christians by our humility, our compassion, our willingness to spend more time with our own sins than with others', our joy in Creation, our loving service of those who are oppressed or denied by this world. Yes, that does happen too. Maybe one of *my* unspoken issues here is the inability to see how much good there is surrounding me.

Saints are *cranky*. If there's any lesson from the remotest past of Christianity, it's that saints can be complete and utter jerks. (Just look at Jerome.) Saints are disputatious. Saints can behave abominably. This is because there is no such thing as a saint or a sinner; we're all real sinners, even the best of us. I gather that Mother Teresa was a real handful. The thing that makes us saints isn't our goodness, God knows; it's our constant, passionate, helpless, indignant wrestling with what this faith-stuff is supposed to be.

I took all this out for a long walk through the beauty of the day; the trees are just turning and the streets are full of color. My own deep anger slid away, replaced by mourning; but the peace of the mild air, the silver of the lake's waters let me be emptied of all that. I came back and made tea and sat down to finish this piece.

I don't like the hymn because it isn't true, and its untruth speaks to how wrongly we've used the great gift of God's grace and Jesus' sacrifice. It's not the hymn's fault that it's untrue. It's ours. Not just ours: mine, for being so angry when it's really up to God to do the judging.

Oh, well. I never said I was a good Christian; I'm not. I'm just still practicing, and I don't expect ever to get it exactly right in this life.

"They'll know we are Christians by our love." Maybe it's just too soon. Maybe I can't take the long-enough view. Maybe there's something out there I don't understand.

Maybe I have to give this hymn another chance.

But next year, *next* year, we are (by God!) going to sing "For All the Saints," or there will be hell to pay.

CHAPTER 6

Lighten Our Darkness

I wait for the Lord, my soul waits
and in his word I hope;
my soul waits for the Lord
more than those who watch
for the morning,
more than those who watch
for the morning.

—PSALM 130:5–6

🌾 The Mourning Dove 🌾

My favorite way into town is from the east, past the quiet suburbs in the military eastern end of town. You come to a T-junction and turn right, passing on your left the stone gardens of Barriefield and on your right the rise of the hill upon which the old stone fort squats, staring intently out over the water, watching for the enemy who never showed up. Pass the military college in its trees at the foot of the fort's glacis, and there's the Cataraqui River, with its calm reed beds, and the causeway with its swing bridge, and then, spread out like something in an old Dutch painting, lies the city.

You see the Roman Catholic cathedral spire, pointing (as Robertson Davies described it) "a vehement and ornate Gothic finger towards Heaven." You see the three domes, of City Hall, the Court House (looking nearer than it actually is), and the Anglican cathedral. Davies fictionalized the cathedral as St. Nicholas and made it an actor in his novels about this city. Its real name is St. George's, and it is one of the most beautiful churches in Canada.

It was begun in 1825, in an elegant late Regency style that beautifully suits the city's silvery limestone. After a fire in 1899, it was rebuilt in its present beauty. I've heard say that it was modeled on St. Paul's Cathedral in London, and it certainly has some of that sense of lightness and airiness—of "offhand Anglican suavity," as Davies puts it. Certainly it is very, very English, right down to the little shaded reading lamps on the choir stalls in the chancel. It is a place, one feels, of immense and unconquerable seemliness, of a steady and placid decency.

It has a shadow side, of course, as all characters must, and its shadow reflects the city's shadow. Kingston, Ontario, where I live, is a city fragmented between elite and underclass; it is a city of universities of the first rank and Canada's worst prisons, of the rich, of modestly prosperous intellectuals, and of the walking wounded. The city's communities—military, prison, university, college, business, bureaucratic, professional—live side by side without ever speaking to each other. Kingston has had a deep, old-fashioned, snobbish Anglophilia that goes well with its beautiful brick and limestone Victorian houses on their tree-shaded streets—although if you go north, the working-class houses are small and shabby, and the neighborhoods are tough indeed. Hell's Angels have firm footholds in both the drug ghetto and in the prosperous suburbs to the west. It's a city of haves and have-nots, and it does not like looking at its own shadow.

The city's Anglican elite went to St. George's. Traditionally, those who worshiped in this lovely building were the cream of the crop, and they knew it. I've heard that until the Second World War, the cathedral's Sunday morning sidesmen, or ushers, appeared in full formal rig, gray gloves and long-tailed morning coats and all, and that intruders from the lower social orders were gently hinted away to other city parishes. I'm not in the least surprised. It was a common enough pattern in Ontario Anglicanism, if one for which I feel no affection whatsoever.

This elitism, and the church's beauty, are both important to this story. But the story is not a beautiful one. Quite the opposite, in fact.

More about beauty. The cathedral had, in the great British tradition, an outstanding men-and-boys choir, the first non-British choir to be invited to perform in Westminster Abbey. The cathedral counted itself lucky, in 1974, to attract one of the finest choirmasters and organists in Canada, a charming, mercurial, charismatic man named John Gallienne—a big bearded man with an overpowering presence. He boosted the already high choral standards for the men-and-boys choir and founded a mixed-voice adult choir and a girls choir that rapidly reached the highest standards and toured Canada and the United States. He and his wife established a vibrant, if alcohol-fueled, social circle composed of the best and brightest. People competed for invitations, or for a weekend at the Galliennes' country cottage. He attracted the more aesthetically enlightened of the city's Anglican population, especially those from the university. He charmed them all.

He charmed them all, while he ate their children.

It was two years after Gallienne arrived that one of the choir boys told his parents that the choirmaster had sexually molested him. Soon after, the boy committed suicide. Gallienne, when challenged, neither admitted nor denied molesting the boy. The matter went no further because the only known complainant was dead. In fact, there were dozens of possible complainants, but none of them was talking. His victims locked away what had been done to them. Some tried to hint about it to their parents, but the parents didn't get the hints, and so the boys concluded that their parents knew and didn't care. Gallienne had them thoroughly under his thumb. He was an outstanding manipulator.

Cathedral officials heard recurring rumors and repeatedly told the parents of the choristers that the situation was well under control. Everyone wanted to believe that. The brilliance of the music dimmed the ears of the adults, clergy, staff, and parents alike. Kids who didn't want to go to choir practice and couldn't explain why were pushed into going by their parents. And so it went on, even after complaints were made to the Children's Aid Society, until a second suicide brought it all to the surface. The parents of both of the dead young men went public. Then, in 1990, after sixteen years of continuous sexual abuse of young boys—his favored victims were eight to eleven years old—the whole horrible mess surfaced. Gallienne pleaded guilty to twenty counts of sexual assault on minors and was sentenced to six years in prison. Nobody really knows how many kids he abused—dozens, at the very least.

The city couldn't believe it. Such a brilliant musician, such a lovely man. There was a great deal of denial at first, and then a huge storm as the cathedral split into factions: those who were fighting for the children, those who were fighting for the choirmaster, and those in the middle who hadn't a clue what to do or think or say. Some didn't believe Gallienne was guilty. Some thought it was no big deal. Some favored forgiving the man and moving on. Some believed that however heinous his crimes, they were redeemed by his musical gifts. Both cathedral and diocese were silent, refusing to accept any responsibility for the problem, although the cathedral had been told repeatedly for more than a decade that there were problems. For two years, worshipers on Sunday morning walked past picketers—their former pew mates—who were calling on the church to take accountability for its failure to protect its most vulnerable members and to issue a formal apology. But the diocese, worried about its legal and financial liability, stalled, and that only fueled the anger.

Even as the cathedral split, so did families. Some parents, believing their children and beginning to understand the damage they had suffered, developed the passionate, appropriate anger that tells the kid that the parent is firmly on his side. They fought like lions to have the abuse addressed and restitution made. Other families didn't. Many simply had no idea what to do. Parents are used to handling cuts and bruises, but how many of us could cope with a serious compound fracture? Some parents knew of the abuse, but couldn't reach their sons, who had locked themselves away with their pain and self-blame. Other parents didn't want to ask, because they were afraid of the answer. There were long, painful silences, which the kids inevitably interpreted as not caring. Silence was like a wedge driven between parent and child.

Or worse, parents knew about the abuse but failed to mourn their children. Instead, they mourned the damage to the music program, the damage to the social circle, the damage to the cathedral's reputation, the damage to the cathedral and diocesan budgets when the lawsuits started. Too many parents did not tell their children that they mourned the damage done to them. Some parents of victims, at Gallienne's sentencing, begged the court to consider his musical gifts and show him mercy.

The children—the ones he'd abused, and their friends and fellow singers who he hadn't touched—watched, and drew their own conclusions. Some walked away. Some got on with their lives. Some went royally off the rails.

The cathedral made efforts toward reconciliation, including paying for a counseling program—for a while. But the diocese's failure to move led to lawsuits against the cathedral and diocese, and the cathedral, panicking over its finances, ended the counseling program. This self-protectiveness, again, only threw fuel on the fire. "So what do you really care about," the children thought, "us or the money?" In the end, the new diocesan bishop made a formal apology to the victims and their families, and the diocese put together a settlement package. People thought that was the end of it.

But as the years passed, the damage lurked beneath the surface, old grief and anger that nobody wanted to acknowledge. Reopening the past looked terribly dangerous, and people had no faith in any possible healing. The cathedral tumbled from crisis to crisis for a decade, losing members steadily. The city looked stony-faced at the cathedral and diocese and thought loud and uncharitable thoughts about responsibility, because the cathedral seemed to feel sorrier for itself than for the victims. Many of Gallienne's victims flamed out or limped along, holding their damage inside themselves in silence as they grew into young men who couldn't talk about the past. For if *he* (their families and community said) was a good man, or at worst a troubled man with a few failings, the problem must be *me*. They carried his evil for him. His supporters had said that Gallienne was the scapegoat, but in fact, the scapegoats were their sons.

Call her Charlotte. I met her through another city choir; we were to sing Bach's Mass in B Minor and both of us were in the tenor section. Before I realized I couldn't manage the music (which is insanely difficult, if beautiful) and dropped out, she and I got together to practice, and we hit it off. She'd been reading my weekly on-line pieces for years.

As we got to be friends, I found out a bit about her life, which had been difficult. Now in her late twenties, she comes from the Queen's University community and is a gifted musician. She has perfect pitch and a huge singing range. She was a brilliant student in school as well, until she was fifteen—and then she turned into every parent's nightmare and made her family's life a perfect hell. After a year she moved out on her own and spent the next few years abusing drugs and alcohol, before finally finding AA and getting herself back on track. There are the faint tracks of cut marks on her arms. But she was on her way back. She'd just finished an undergraduate degree in math and philosophy. When I met her, she was in her first year at Queen's Law School. She takes all the lawyer jokes with a redheaded broad's big, warm grin. She has a true vocation for the law, and it is her delight. She is vibrant and passionate and full of joy.

We got to be closer friends when, almost simultaneously, our marriages both failed and we found ourselves hip-deep in unpacking our own emotional baggage—we both have messy pasts, in different ways. It was good to have company in the process. We'd get together for coffee at our favorite downtown place, the Sleepless Goat, and compare notes on our complete mental and emotional depletion as we worked through what had happened, and why, and what our own parts were. We could sit companionably with each other as chunks of old pain, frozen like dry ice, rose to the surface and melted into the spring air.

I was to meet her for coffee at the Goat one Saturday afternoon in May and stopped to buy the papers. The city paper had a front-page story: Gallienne was conducting choir and playing the organ at a church in Ottawa, in abrogation of an agreement imposed by the bishop when Gallienne was paroled. The bishop here had forbidden him from taking any leadership role in a church, and the bishop of Ottawa had agreed to the ban. But the rector of Gallienne's parish disagreed, feeling that he'd done his time and his gifts were valuable to the parish. It was, the rector said, a question of human rights.

When I got to the Goat, Charlotte was already there. She sat over her coffee, her brilliant blue eyes wide open but unseeing. She'd seen the story, and it had knocked the wind right out of her. She could barely talk, and she's usually a highly articulate young woman. Phrases dropped out of her, disconnected.

She had been a founding member of Gallienne's girls choir. He had discovered her perfect pitch, coached her singing, taken her and the rest of the choir on tour. Her parents were in that delightful well-lubricated social circle.

Just after the scandal broke, when she was fourteen, she came home one day to find Gallienne sitting in her parents' living room. Her parents "didn't want to take sides." But silence, especially to a child, can look very much like collusion.

She had never, up to that May afternoon, made the connection between Gallienne and her own crash-and-burn period. Now she did.

"Time heals all wounds." Well, I suppose in one sense that's true; in a thousand years, everyone concerned in this story will be long dead and gone and the cathedral itself (being built of limestone) will have vanished away. But a mere couple of decades won't heal wounds when they are this deep and this septic. The infection merely encysts. That the infection is still very much there was clear from the vehement reaction that some (not all) of the cathedral people had to the newspaper story. A healed wound isn't that sore to the touch. They were furiously angry: "Why did the paper have to dredge this up again? Hasn't he paid his dues? What about forgiveness?"

Forgiveness matters hugely. Forgiveness would be all well and good if the healing had truly happened, if we'd drained the abscess, emptied out the toxins. To change metaphors, if the cathedral scandal was a can of worms, we needed to empty the can out, give it a good wash, and set it up on the mantlepiece clean, as a memorial to the victims. But that's not what happened, all those years ago. What happened instead was silencing: "We've done this work. It's over. We're going to move on and not talk about this any more. We will not speak of this again."

But silencing shames the victims, forcing them to internalize the evil that has been done to them instead of handing it back to the offender, to whom it properly belongs: "Here; this isn't mine, it's yours." This hasn't happened here. Instead, there has been far too much silence, and far too much denial. Denial re-victimizes the victims, dismissing what happened to them. There wasn't one victimizer at the cathedral; there were many.

Since none of this was acknowledged, since the trauma to the kids was denied and minimized, the process of real forgiveness got short-circuited. It is possible to forgive someone who denies any wrong-doing, but it's extremely difficult, and the deeper the denial, the tougher the process. The denial, when it digs in deep, becomes itself a sin of the first order.

There were two separate narratives—the primary and secondary victims on one hand and the cathedral on the other, and they could not hear each other. The process of forgiveness had seized up.

The not-hearing has (I believe) to do with a fundamental error in confusing hurt with trauma. We all get hurt; it's part of the human condition. Life is full, it seems, of elbows and corners, and it behooves us as adults to develop a reasonably tough hide and learn to accept hurt, deal with it appropriately (which does not mean pretending it doesn't exist), and come to terms with it. Healing is very real.

The cathedral had been hurt, badly hurt—no doubt about that at all. That was its narrative. But the cathedral kids' narrative was different. They hadn't just been hurt; they'd been traumatized. Their world had been turned upside down. What happened to them was not normal, in-the-scheme-of-things owwies, but betrayal at the most fundamental level, where sexuality and spirituality meet in the depths of the human soul, where the child exists in a deep relationship with its parents and community, in the trustable certainty of care—and above all, where the child lives with God. There had been a huge unintended but real betrayal of the child's trust in his or her personal home place. This had never been properly acknowledged. You can get over hurt; trauma requires another type of processing.

I found myself struggling with, trying to make sense of all this, to find its meaning. To deal with Charlotte and to help her untangle all those ancient brambles in which I found myself (also) enmeshed, I needed to understand all this. I spent many hours reading up on the case, talking to people who were close to it at the time. It seemed important to me to get the facts correct, to evaluate fairly, to see without rushing to judgment—but also to hold this in one hand and the Gospel in the other and look back and forth between them. For the cathedral, besides being a musical institution and a social group, is also a church, and a church is supposed to walk in the Kingdom way, although sadly many seem to wander off in other directions.

The Kingdom way, in facing oppression, is to stand with the oppressed and resist the oppressor. The Kingdom way, in dealing with injustice, is to confront the injustice and bring it to an end.

Charlotte knew, as I did, that the Kingdom way of dealing with someone who sexually exploits children should have been for the community to go in like a whole pride of lions, roaring, "We don't care if you're Johann Sebastian Bach reincarnated; you *do not* harm our children!"

I am older than Charlotte, and I can see how adults don't always understand with the clarity that children do and how they get muddled by factors that seem, to the kids, to be wholly irrelevant. But I'm also a parent, and I know that what matters most is the message that the adults send the kids. The message the kids had received was the wrong message, and that again re-traumatized them.

But at the same time, I couldn't sit in judgment on the cathedral, and especially not on the families. As a parent, I have not always practiced what I preached, and my kids have suffered for that. I too have made mistakes, usually more of omission than commission, but does it really matter which it is? I know what it's like to watch one's own child struggling—stuck, unreachable, unapproachable—and simply not know what to do. Sometimes, everything you do as a parent just seems to make it all worse. There is nothing more baffling, painful, or disheartening. There is nothing more terrifying or inducive of the most gut-wrenching guilt.

I walked with Charlotte through her old grief and anger— but I also heard from cathedral people who feel that they never have been and never will be forgiven, no matter what they do or say. No penitence is apparently enough.

I thought about flaws and pressures. Not one of us, individual or family or institution, isn't human and therefore flawed. Some children are more sensitive, introverted, and strongly spiritual than others, and they are more at risk in this type of situation. Some families might be flat-out dysfunctional, but others may have patterns that are fine for one child and not good for another.

If the cathedral had its flaws, find me a human institution that doesn't. It was the combination of all these things, brought under crushing pressure by Gallienne and his spectacular manipulation, that led to the tragedy.

Assigning blame isn't my job under the circumstances. I can't. That's God's job, not mine. Pointing one finger at the cathedral points three fingers back at me.

I wrestled with all this, and also tried both to write my way through it and to help Charlotte as she struggled with memories, with anger, with the sense that her world had betrayed her—and above all, with the damage to her spiritual life, for that fifteen-year-old was a girl of extraordinarily strong spirituality and idealism. This strength of hers was badly betrayed by those who should have nurtured it. So badly betrayed, in fact, that it turned and stabbed her in the side. Oh, those were dark days.

This darkness, added to all the other darkness in the world these days, sometimes seemed overwhelming. I knew I needed to take a break from it, to gain a little perspective. I've learned in such cases that what's generally useful is to get my feet on the earth, open my eyes and ears, and be ready to take in whatever Creation might have to whisper to me. So, a couple of Saturdays later, I put my sandals on and went off for a walk in the park.

The lilacs were out. The city has so many lilacs that the air was full of scent. It was full of city birds as well: glossy crows and starlings, swallows swooping after bugs, the ubiquitous gulls and sparrows, and elegant, streamlined gray mourning doves. We have a lot of these doves in my neighborhood. As I crossed into the park, one flew up and lighted on an overhead telephone wire. I paused to look up at it, hoping to hear it call, because I love the sound and needed to hear it just now. The bird obliged; as I stood with my toes in the longish grass, I heard its distinctive soft, piercing croon, the call that earned the bird its popular name.

The call always makes me think of old sorrow—sorrow puri-fied of all anger or bitterness, sorrow even purified of pain, sorrow double-distilled into its truest self. Sorrow that sits with those who are suffering, not saying anything much, not trying to explain or excuse or justify or set them to rights, but simply keeping them company and listening with all its loving attention and tending to the wounds, and handing a clean handkerchief when needed.

It takes patience. Even quite ordinary wounds take a variable length of time to heal, and the process cannot be rushed. Job's comforters lost patience; they wanted him to get over it *now* so they could escape the discomfort of sitting in silence with him. They found themselves having to argue him out of his suffering, having to justify it, desiring to fill the emptiness with words not for his sake but for their own. Sitting with it in quietness was, they found, too much for them. Not surprising; it's often too much for us. It's often too much for us to sit quietly with our own suffering, after all.

But it's what needs to be done, and what we had not done.

We all collectively failed to do that for the cathedral victims. We did not sit quietly with them, accepting their suffering, letting them empty it out completely so that the space in them could be refilled with grace and love and healing. This failure of ours is a crying sin.

But as I stood in the lilac-scented, bird-songed quietness of the day, something came to me: a vision of something happening just past the skin of things, where the deeper realities play and tumble in a cleaner air than I have ever breathed. I knew suddenly that God, seeing the place next to each one of them vacant, slipped into it, taking on the work of mourning. I could trust that God will, in the fullness of time, set all this mess to rights, mending the victims, mending the victimizers. Suddenly, standing in the park with Creation wrapped around me in all its early summer beauty,

I knew with gut certainty that, yes, in God's own time, this will indeed happen. For in God's own time, the Kingdom way will prevail, and all will be led home, "and God will wipe away every tear from their eyes."

The cathedral is a chastened place these days. It now offers a daily lunch for the poor of the city, an important service. It's attracted some new young families and there is a small Sunday school. A couple of years ago, it rededicated the chapel to the spirit of reconciliation and healing. There is talk about putting up a plaque in memory of all Gallienne's victims, and that would be a good thing to do.

Charlotte and I still meet at the Goat to talk, but we talk less about Gallienne as the weeks pass and she does her own inner work. She comes, nowadays, to the quiet Thursday Eucharist at my church, where there is no music, only times of refreshing silence. It does her good, she says.

(For all of John Gallienne's victims, primary, secondary, and tertiary, and in memory of Henrik Helmers and Tim Franks. Their souls have found peace in God's healing care.)

❧ Floomph ❧

It happened about three or four days into the flu, while I was still in the annoying shivery and sweating phase. One moment I was a person of faith; the next moment, the whole thing—my whole edifice of belief—folded, collapsing like one of those old-fashioned yellow canvas tents falling in on itself under a rainstorm. Floomph; and there it was, a soggy heap on the ground.

I stared at the mess, knowing I didn't have the strength so much as to pull the heavy wet folds straight, much less sort out the mess and put the thing back up. "Well, God, I'm sorry," I muttered, and curled up and got on with the shivers and sweats and coughing.

Oh, I knew that this faith collapse had everything to do with influenza and its consequent exhaustion, and probably a fair bit with long-term stress. I'd been riding for a spiritual fall for quite a while. I know in my head that God's absence from my life is apparent, not real, and short-term, not long-term; and it says nothing whatsoever about God's existence. I lay there in the arms of flu and my Maker and whispered, "Just because I can't feel you doesn't mean you aren't real."

Knowing that this is an artifact of flu and stress does not, however, help much. It still feels like a hole in a back molar, the kind of vastly empty achiness that you could park a truck in. I can say to myself that God's still out there, even if I can't feel God anywhere, but my human nature starts muttering about "imaginary feel-good stuff" and "comforting self-delusion," and I don't have the spiritual wherewithal to argue back.

The problem with a state like this is that as long as you're in it, you really can't imagine being otherwise. Not only does faith go floomph, but it feels as though faith has always been, and will always be, in that discouraging condition. It makes you realize how little this whole business has to do with logic and cognition. If I could reason myself into a state of belief, I'd do just that, for the certainty and comfort of it.

But faith is the springing of something deep within the soul, leaping Godward. If this something loses its spring and falls flat on its tush, no Thomistic power of reasoning is going to help one lousy little bit. If I can't find God anywhere in the landscape around me, I'm sure as heck not going to find him in a syllogism, however impeccable. Sigh.

Maybe it's an Advent thing. Maybe I'm just supposed to sit here quietly, hands upturned and empty, waiting, just as the world waited two thousand years ago for the baby who was to bring earth and God together in one small, puling body. Maybe this isn't so much a collapse as an emptying out, a part of becoming ready for something still to come, like cleaning out my purse before I go on a journey. Maybe God needs to be out of my life for a while for reasons that I don't understand, but that God does.

While I was in spiritual floomphishness, the landscape around me was in mud season at its level worst. The days were growing shorter, the skies held gray, and rain fell in a cold, desultory way. I have long since learned to accept that this is a normal part of the Canadian seasonal spin, perhaps one of the least lovable times of year, but having its own definite term and place in the cycle. Maybe I can accept that spiritual mud season is also a natural and inevitable part of the Journey—by no means entertaining, but simply one of those things you go through, and eventually come out the other end.

One thing I do know: this emptiness will pass. If it's just flu, stress, and fatigue, it will ease as I start to recover. If it's an Advent emptying out, God will again fill the God-shaped hole in God's good time. Maybe not as fast as I'd like, but that's good for my patience. It's just a matter of waiting it out, and drinking lots of water and getting enough rest, and being willing to wander the wilderness for however many laps is good.

I heard some particularly lovely plainsong chant on the radio, and I found I could sort of lean up against it, if you know what I mean, and take some secondhand comfort from the faith of those who wrote this beauty, however hollow and empty my own particular cupboard feels. I found a ladybug on my desk, slow to the point of paralysis but still alive when I puffed gently at it, and I could take a scrap of my old dear joy in God's creation in this burnished, richly red-brown spotted carapace. I can still whisper the Lord's Prayer; the child's things-of-faith hang on and help carry the stumbling adult through the dry desert spaces. The fat old hymns still move me to smile. The hunger's still there, the ache that only God can soothe. That's got to be worth something.

❧ The Callus ❧

The callus on the tip of my left index finger has broken down.

I think you need to be someone who plays (or, like me, attempts to play) a stringed instrument to understand what this means, or why it matters. The stringed instrument in my case (pun somewhat intended) is a guitar, one of which I am wholly unworthy but which graces my life nonetheless. She's a big, beautiful Gibson, passed on to me by my kid sister. She deserves someone better at guitar playing than I am, but I'm who she has for now: her person, imperfect but appreciative.

If you play a guitar, your left hand presses down on the strings to vary their pitch while your right hand strikes, strums, plucks, or just plain fumbles to make the thing produce sound, amounting to music if you know roughly what you're doing. Left-hand fingertips get callused by all that string-pressing-down, especially when the strings are steel, as my guitar's strings are. Developing calluses is a good thing if you're playing the guitar; your tone is much clearer when you aren't wincing with pain. Having the callus on a fingertip suddenly start to disintegrate and peel away, as mine did on Tuesday, is a pain in the E-string. It's not just that it hurts; it's that the relics of the callus tend to catch on the string, which is slightly maddening.

Calluses can be extremely useful things. When I was a child, running barefoot all summer long, the soles of my feet grew so tough that my mother, at summer's end, could sit down with a young foot in one hand and a needle in the other and take out splinters without my so much as whimpering. I didn't feel a thing. Anyone in serious manual work develops the hand-toughness to handle bricks or raw cod or a gardening spade without the hands cracking, hurting, and starting to bleed.

We need calluses because our toes and fingers, the soles of our feet, and the palms of our hands—which are where we tend to develop them—are so incredibly sensitive. They convey essential touch information to the brain, the more so since we are upright-walking, tool-making animals. It's one of those paradoxes that these twenty small bits of body, these digit tips, are so packed with nerve endings that they can detect the pressure of two pins a millimeter apart. When I play (say) an Am7 chord, the pressure that the strings exert on this so-sensitive flesh must be unspeakable—think of the forces involved and the area of the string and you get the picture. Somehow my fingertips have to get tough enough to manage, and they do, just as a ballerina's toes have to learn to accommodate the full weight of her body when she's dancing *en pointe*. The physics of this stuff is mind-boggling.

The heart too has to learn how to manage. The small city where I live is full of broken people. The psych hospital has cut its beds from seventeen hundred to fewer than two hundred, and a lot of the former patients are wandering around downtown. Between them and the human flotsam from the prison system, the poor, the halt, the blind, the lame, and the extremely eccentric, downtown is full of broken people with faces that make your eyes skitter away in search of something less challenging.

How can you live in this world *without* a callused heart? How can you regard the suffering around even this pretty, pleasant, comfortable small city without being wrenched? That's not even to begin imagining the suffering elsewhere: the suffering of Iraq before, during, and after this war; the immense suffering in the lands hit by tsunamis, the Congo and Sudan, Somalia, the

Palestinian camps, North Korea. We can't begin to look at the human condition with any clarity at all without hurting just as much as an uncalloused fingertip pressing down on that top E-string, the thinnest and sharpest of all.

On the one hand, we're called to love our neighbor, with no set limits on who that neighbor is, whether it's the floridly psychotic woman in crazy clothes singing to herself at the corner of Princess and Wellington, or the boy in the Baghdad hospital missing limbs and family, or the beautiful Sudanese women lining up for water in a refugee camp and watching their children starve. On the other hand, if we take on all the suffering of the world, we'll never get anything accomplished. We'll be crushed.

I'm feeling my way through this particular maze these days as I wander around downtown, with its lovely silvery limestone buildings, its boutiques and restaurants, and its wild mixture of people. I have never, I think, been so conscious of both the beauty of this world and its brokenness, and sometimes the brokenness feels sharp as jagged glass.

It's hard, after living in a small town for sixteen years, to walk past a beggar, neither ignoring him nor getting drawn into her toils. I can do so only because I also know that social services here are really pretty good, and the town itself has an undertow of courtesy and compassion. There are much worse places to be broken than this one. For starters, craziness isn't considered exceptional here, and that alone makes it easier to live with.

It's always tricky, managing to keep enough callus on your guitar-playing fingertips to manage a D chord without flinching while, at the same time, retaining enough feeling to manage the delicate tasks that need those fingertips' full participation. It's tricky accepting this world's brokenness without losing the need to fight for justice. It's tricky managing compassion and common sense. But nobody said that living would ever be easy, especially if you're trying to be loving too.

Only God can hold all this suffering in God's heart and meet it with infinite love and understanding. I can't reflect this, except in the smallest ways—but that doesn't mean I should accept my own limitations. I should struggle to stretch myself, to find ways of ministering to others with compassion *and* with common sense. I know the hard way in which compassion without common sense ends up wasting the compassion without doing any practical good. But common sense without compassion can so easily slip into the sort of self-satisfied cruelty that pretends others' suffering isn't real at all. It is, oh God: it is.

Above all, I have to remember two things. First, I am a sinner, and I necessarily fail in this loving-God-and-neighbor bit, although that does not let me off the hook for doing what I can. Second, staying in consciousness of this world's suffering and praying about it is, in fact, one part of the work, and a good and important part.

I filed off the roughest bits of my ex-callus with an emery board, gently. I've rubbed a little hand cream on, and I'm back to playing, trying to build up that tough skin again. It will take a few days, I suppose.

❧ French Suites ☙

I cannot for the life of me face listening to the 2:00 p.m. news on the radio as I drive. It's just all too much—the unspeakable abuse of Iraqi prisoners, Israeli-Palestinian conflicts, the simmering chaos in Africa, stupidity of all sorts, clearly laying up a whole pack of trouble. All over the map these days, people are choosing to treat other people as things, unworthy of ordinary decency—worthy, in fact, of extraordinary indecency—and of course it will all turn out so much the worse in the end.

It's hard to believe in the possibility of peace these days, hard to see how God might be at work. It seems as though we keep grasping at our ideals of (say) international cooperation and community, and then something happens like the Iraq war, and then we're back to square one, or even back to square minus fifteen, which is what Iraq feels like to me these days. I cannot accept that the ends justify the means. They never do, after all. There is expediency and there is the Kingdom way, and I can't accept choosing the first over the second, especially when someone else must pay the price. As always someone must.

Life's troubling enough without having to endure hearing about things I cannot do anything about, at least not immediately. So I find the button for the CD player in my new-to-me car and touch it, and the news disappears. In its place, sanity pours through the speakers.

I have put on a CD of Bach's French Suites for keyboard. This performance is on piano and not particularly good; I really must replace it. Nonetheless, it's good old Johann Sebastian: steady, rational, comforting, speaking deeply of civilized assumptions and values I can appreciate. I've always thought it isn't that God has to justify God's ways to humans; humans need to justify their ways to God, and Bach's music goes some way to doing so. For me, this music is sanity time.

But I'm also aware of the fact that Bach's life was, in fact, full of conflict and suffering: the early loss of siblings and parents, the death of his first wife and many of his children, constant job woes (many of them self-inflicted; the man had a temper and a strong sense of self-importance). All this against the background of court squabbles, in a landscape torn to shreds in his grandparents' time by a hideous civil war, with other wars marching back and forth across the continent throughout his lifetime. It was not a quiet time then either. It's just that this particular music doesn't talk about it.

Suffering is nothing new. It happens all around us, with or without our being aware of it. It happens in us, because inevitably life bruises us and we have to come to terms with that. Also, we need to struggle with our own part in the bruising, the way in which we have "followed too much the devices and desires of our own hearts." If we don't deal with our own suffering—and many don't; many turn away from it or try to bury it or numb themselves out from it—all we do is postpone it to the future, or inflict it on other people. Suffering *is*; the question (as always) is, What are we going to do with it? What are we going to let it make of us?

I turn back to the music for solace, for the dream of innocence. I'm not going to find either of them in the world of humankind these days, or so it seems at the moment. I cannot remember a darker time since the late 1960s. This time has that same nightmarish feel to it. God and the prospect of peace both feel very far away from the face of the earth at this moment.

But it's not really an option, innocence. I can't turn away from this world's suffering and escape into the music. I'd lose too much if I tried that. I know, because I've tried in the past and I've watched others do the same. I could try to vanish into these French Suites, as another might disappear into (say) sitcoms or Scotch or sex, in order to dampen my own anxiety, turning my back on what I don't feel I can manage. But this means turning my back on too much other stuff: the needs of the people I love, my own need for wholeness and integration, and also the swoop and twitter of swallows bug hunting at the water's edge, the sound of a mourning dove, the scent of wild lilac or of sheets dried on the line. To turn your back on the world's suffering is also to turn away from its beauty.

I can't turn away, either, because if I do, I am refusing to sit with others' suffering and actually do something about it—proclaim what's going on, stand up against it, shout out how wrong it is, or at the very least sit quietly in empathy with it.

We have to take this world as God takes us, bright and dark together. Somehow we have to find ways both of challenging the darkness and of discovering where the brightness lies. But above all we must never deny the reality and profundity of the suffering in ourselves and others. By turning our backs on it, we turn our backs on God, who sits with those who suffer.

Here it comes, the gigue to the fifth French Suite, my fave. The opening notes leap and skitter like flecks of light exploding upward, and the second voice of the fugue comes whipping in, chasing the upper line, both of them laughing, and then the third voice and the fourth, and suddenly it's turned into a tag team of pure joy. I used to dislike it when, in the second part of the piece, Bach flipped the theme on its head and turned it into depth and darkness, but as I grow older I'm willing to see that the two need each other, and that they bring each other ultimately to peace and completion.

So it goes. I have faith that ultimately things *will* come to peace and completion, although probably not in my time. All I can do is live as best I can without turning away from reality in search of innocence, and to love as best I can this world, exactly the way it is.

✵ Lights in the Wilderness ✵

Once, in early winter, I had a speaking gig in southwestern Missouri, hosted by a wealthy Episcopalian church there. I flew into and out of O'Hare Airport in Chicago. It was dusk as we left, a cloudless evening. The darkness deepened as we flew south and west over Illinois. I looked down out the window and there below us St. Louis spread out, a glittering mass slashed through with the great black lines of the Mississippi and Missouri Rivers as they converged.

As we crossed Missouri, I saw town after town, village after village, farm after farm, forming a dense, lacy pattern of light, punctuated by small spaces of dark and the occasional larger town. It struck me, looking down, how thoroughly populated the country was—not surprising; much of Missouri is good farmland. We saw the larger light mass of Springfield and began to make our landing.

Three days later, after my talks and some very good time with some dear and loving friends, I flew home again, again at dusk, again through O'Hare, heading north and east. But this time the evening was cloudy. I saw only the huge light mass of Chicago and a glimpse of Lake Michigan, and then nothing. I turned back to my book and read for an hour or so.

When I looked out the window again, we were in clear skies and obviously in Canada. I could tell that by the thin double line of light running east-north-east with a narrow strip of blackness in between and blackness, dotted with the occasional light, stretching off to the north, indefinitely. We were flying over the settled strip alongside the St. Lawrence River. It's not the Golden Horseshoe (the heavily settled southwestern tip of Ontario), but it's not exactly the back of beyond either. Not by Canadian standards.

I thought of the time I went camping on Manitoulin Island, and I got the merest hint of a suggestion of the size and unpopulated emptiness of Northern Ontario—a thousand miles of woods with only the barest sprinkling of tiny settlements and the occasional small town. And that's Ontario; Northern Quebec is even bigger. If you're Canadian, you live always with the small tug of consciousness of the North, the *real* North, where the tiny community lights would be like a handful of bright beads tossed over an acre of black.

Lights in the darkness. "Lighten our darkness, we beseech thee, O Lord," an ancient and beautiful Anglican prayer begins. At Epiphany, the Feast of Light, in the northern part of the Northern hemisphere, we're just barely beginning to turn around from the darkest time of the year.

Now, there's darkness and then there's darkness; not all darkness is created equal. Darkness can be the foil that sets off the sparkle of gold. During Christmas, for example, the dark is supposed to sparkle with anticipation; it's supposed to be alive with whispering and the occasional giggle, the electric blue at dusk, crisp with fresh snow. Then it's supposed to explode into brilliance and rejoicing, the splendor of gold and scarlet and royal blue, the strong formal harmonies of excellent music, the richness and solemnity of Midnight Mass, the happiness of Christmas morning. If all goes well, that is, and sometimes it does.

There is the darkness of mystery, the cloud of unknowing, the dark that reminds us that we cannot get God completely taped. This is a darkness of majesty and authority, and all I can do is stand before it in wonder and awe. I don't have any problem with that darkness at all.

There is the warm and loving darkness of being held safe and trusting in the palm of God's hand. I've always felt that maybe we need a period of quiet darkness after we cross the River into the Life to Come, a time of being held and healed—almost like the close, nurturing dark of the womb. But I don't know. That's the thing about this death business; it's always a guessing game.

But there is human darkness as well, and it is not good darkness. There's the darkness that we choose to walk right into when we turn away from walking Godward. It doesn't have to be evil, although sometimes it ends up heading that way. It can, instead, be a darkness of hardness, unlovingness, pride, anger, rigid independence. Or it can be the darkness of deception and self-deception, the darkness that we enter (paradoxically) by refusing to accept our own shadow.

I've been spending some time lately contemplating another sort of darkness, one that Elizabeth Goudge describes, a darkness of the spirit: "Through the years her faith had grown so strong that she had not believed that she could lose it. The living light that had made love possible had seemed too glorious ever to go out, yet now it had gone and left her in darkness, and the loneliness of life without love was to her a horror quite indescribable. . . . It had been for nothing, she thought. It was not true. It had been for nothing."

It always drives me a little nuts when someone says, "If God feels very far away, who moved?" Yes, the answer is obvious, but sometimes it's not so much that we moved as we were pushed. Too much stress over too long a time, too big a loss or series of losses, too many prayers gone apparently unanswered, or answered in ways that we don't like, and it begins to feel as though we're walking in the dark, stumbling through a landscape utterly devoid of light.

How can we deal with this darkness? We all encounter it, I'm sure, at one stage or another. It's nothing less than the collapse of faith, and it is about as entertaining as a root canal.

The answer, it seems to me, lies in trust.

We have to trust others to be the light to us. People in the real North don't live in isolation; they live in small, close-knit communities with very strong ties. Without community, they could not survive. It's hard, when you're stumbling around like a complete idiot in the dark, crashing into the furniture and breaking the odd knickknack, to accept the loving light of others. We're too ashamed of our own darkness and weakness. If we've suffered trust wounds in the past, it's even harder. But we have to do it. If the Trinity tells us anything, it tells us about community, relatedness, the necessary interweaving of love among us.

We have to trust in our own humanity. For people who take this God business seriously, this seems to be particularly difficult. The Goudge character who expressed such utter desolation realizes in time that a large part of her spiritual problem is simple exhaustion. Sometimes we need to take ourselves off the hook, sit down, put our feet up, and realize that too much stress and fatigue take a physical toll. Mind and body are too closely related for one not to affect the other.

We have to trust in the Epiphany. Yes, Christmas came and went, and there was a horrible earthquake in Iran that killed tens of thousands of people. Tectonic plates continue to slither around, and disasters like these will be an inevitable part of life as long as this earth exists. Christmas came and went, and the fighting went on in Iraq and the Middle East. Human beings will continue to cling to their grudges and hatred—maybe not forever, but I'm not expecting it to end anytime soon. Christmas has come and gone, and poverty and oppression remain; we can chew away at them, and we *do* chew away at them, one nibble at a time, but there's still so far to go.

But Epiphany comes every year, whatever state we're in. We can trust in that.

Even when the darkness feels very thick indeed, there's a spark of light: God loved us so much that He volunteered to come into our darkness and be with us here. I will take that as the tiny spark of steel on flint, and will I feed it tinder and build it into stronger and steadier light, and I will try my best to take that light and carry it out to those who still walk in darkness.

> *The people that walked in darkness*
> *have seen a great light;*
> *those who lived in a land of deep darkness—*
> *on them light has shined.*

Isaiah 9:2 was right. It shines again in this Epiphany: light and the promise of light.

(Epiphany 2004)

CHAPTER 7

Last Things

For you do not give me up to Sheol,
or let your faithful one see
the Pit.
You show me the path of life.
In your presence there is
fullness of joy;
in your right hand are pleasures
forevermore.

—PSALM 16:10–11

✿ Princess Pine ✿

Here it is again, a soft mat to sink my toes into: princess pine. I wasn't expecting to find it here. But at least this time, I know what to call it.

I've known and loved the plant itself for more than forty years now, but I didn't learn the name of it until one summer when I was camping in the Adirondacks in northern New York State and went to visit the gorgeous nature center in the village of Paul Smiths. I'd seen a carpet of the plant at the center, and I briefly slipped my sandals off to dig my toes in, as I loved doing all those years ago, back in my own particular mountains.

The plant fascinated me back then: it looked so much like a tiny pine tree, only an inch or two long. I figured it for something in the moss department, because it tended to grow in places where I would expect moss, and also because it was so odd, not like any other plant I'd ever seen. It formed mats that felt like nature's answer to the deepest, most luscious plush carpet, the sort you cannot possibly afford. I always wanted to know what it was.

This time (hallelujah!) I had both the plant itself and naturalists within easy reach. I pulled up one of the plants—although they have a deep taproot, they hold so lightly to the soil that you can pull a plant out without breaking it—and holding it in the palm of my hand I went to look for instruction.

Not a moss, I was told; a pine. *The* ancestral pine, in fact: the ur-pine, and very ancient indeed. The naturalist told me the Latin name, which, of course, I immediately forgot. The common name is princess pine. Princess pine: there. Me, I'd have come up with something more poetic, but princess pine would do as a name. That very old itch scratched at last.

I first found princess pine the same moment I found God, as a barefoot child on the Oxbow Road in Heath, in the depths (or heights) of the Massachusetts Berkshires. I felt it under my bare brown childish toes as I looked deep down into the woods, knowing that somewhere over the next ridge there was a Someone who spoke to me with such deep gentle knowledge, who loved and treasured me as I'd never been loved and treasured before. My toes went down into the soft, damp kindness of princess pine, and tenderness seemed to flow up from it into all the sorenesses and loneliness inside me. I learned in that moment the knack of finding a single pulse of joy, of staying in it while time stretched and bent around me, of wrapping up the moment in the amber of memory, to be stored away, so I could always go back to it when I needed to.

I also learned to look for and treasure whatever patches of the plant I could come across, because the feel of it under my feet took me back to that moment. There was a particularly delicious patch, unusually deep, outside the door into the lower level of our barn, where the wood pile was. Whenever I was sent to get a barrow of wood for the fireplace and Franklin stove, I'd always pause there to dig my toes into the cool, damp softness and be refreshed.

Then I moved away from the mountains: to Iowa, and then to Canada. Princess pine surely grows in places like the Gaspé Peninsula and Nova Scotia and the Canadian Shield somewhere, but I haven't seen any, possibly because I don't expect to; it's still an Appalachian thing for me. I learned to live without it.

But here it was again, in the churchyard of my mother's long-time parish, under a cool gray sky. I wanted to slip my shoes off and dig my toes in, but it wasn't that sort of occasion. My sister and I walked companionably quiet, through the young verdure, past a double row of pear tree saplings, to a rough place of pine trees, wild blueberry plants, and (incongruously) one extremely cheerful daffodil. This is where parishioners' ashes get buried. We were looking for a suitable spot for our mother.

We found one, under the wild blueberries and within close sight of the daffodils, and fetched the parish's sexton, who marked the spot. Two days later, we and our older sister and the grand-children poured her ashes into the hole he'd dug and trickled in handfuls of the loose, sandy soil. And that was that.

Except that it isn't, because on the other side of the River my mother lives again, but renewed—all the pain and soul damage not just ended but transmuted into glory. She was always excellent at figuring out what to do with suffering—God knows, she had enough practice!—and now all the practice is made perfect. All her roughnesses and failings God will unravel and knit up again the way she should have been, if this world had been a perfect place for her instead of one wracked with fissures and failures. There she will meet and be truly loved by all those whose love for her was so faulty and damaging. There her weaknesses, that in their turn caused so much hurt and damage, will be put to rights. All her real strengths—her flaming intelligence, her insight, her deep love of God, her spiritual discipline—will simply grow until they stretch from one star to another, from galaxy to galaxy.

I plan on finding princess pine on the other shore; I refuse to believe that something so blessed for me in this life will be lack-ing in the next. Whatever C. S. Lewis may have written in *The Great Divorce* about the diamond-hard grass of Heaven, I am per-suaded that the ground there will be gentle under our feet; we will be wrapped about with tenderness, as well as clarity and insight. Then we can face who we have truly been and what we have truly done, because we'll be so safely held in the hands of love that there will be no fear to make us stubbornly blind.

When I cross, she'll rise up to meet me, and our own long damage will be made good.

Now I have to learn how to grieve her. It's easy for me to grieve the lesser, easier loves—a cat, a house, a town, a bloke; inso-far as they had their grief and problems (not the cat!) at least the problems weren't foundational to the way my life has gone. It is not easy for me to grieve my parents; the relationships were too knotty, the love between and among us too important and too seriously flawed. In the days around my parents' deaths, mysteries opened up to me and I saw clearly and irrefutably what the patterns had been, and how they had shaped my choices, for good and ill.

There's work between where I am now and where grief will be, a whole lot of work: work of understanding, of anger and forgiveness. It's OK. Work never bothers me much, as long as I can get on with it. This is where I go next.

So on a cloudy morning in May, as my sister and I walked back between the pear saplings, I pulled a single stalk of princess pine on my way back to the car, turning it between my fingers, remembering the promise, trusting it, believing it. We will be set to rights in God's good time, and then there really will be joy everlasting.

(In memory of Barbara Buckley Wolf, April 25, 1924–May 12, 2003)

✵ Auld Acquaintance ✵

I walked out to the mall along what used to be the path and is now a graveled right-of-way, where they dug the water, sewer, electrical, and gas lines. I'm glad to see, however, that the flowering weeds are slowly closing in, finding a foothold; the gravel part is narrower than it was. Good. I always like to see the weeds win.

Most of the wild flowers are done now that it's the end of September; all that's left, really, are the asters, Queen Anne's lace, a few black-eyed susans, some butter-and-eggs. It's been a slow, late fall, for all the dry weather; the trees are still green and people's flower gardens are surprisingly bright and lively. Nonetheless, it's getting to be autumn: the air is cooler, evenings are distressingly short, and the greenery has taken on a weary, washed-out look as the chloroplasts start to pack it in, having done their work.

I too am feeling nearly autumnal. Yesterday, at a literary event, I saw an old acquaintance for the first time in what must be at least six years. This is someone I've known since college days, although we rarely see each other. When we first met, we were both leggy youngsters of eighteen. Now it's (aiee!) closing in on forty years later. I don't see a whole lot of aging in my own mirror, probably because I'm so used to my mug that I don't notice how it's weathering; I do notice, however, that hoisting myself up from sitting on the floor has turned into a slow, painstaking, achy sort of business. But my old acquaintance looks a *lot* older than he did the last time I saw him—not old yet, but clearly on the slope toward age. We are both in life as the season is in the cycle of the year: well past summer and heading inexorably into fall.

I never thought I'd live much past sixty; life was sufficiently difficult that I figured I'd burn out and crash young. All I had in mind was getting my younger kid to twenty-one and then, I thought, I could afford to pack it in. I never made much provision for growing old, any more than a child makes provision for the end of summer.

But this last summer, I made some changes to the way I live, and these changes significantly increase the chance that I will grow old. It's not a total certainty, of course; I could still step out in front of a bus or be felled by West Nile virus (or more likely the flu). There is, however, a greater likelihood of my hanging around to give my kids something to worry about in their middle age, as though there weren't enough already for middle-aged people to worry about.

I hope I find, as I get closer to old age, that I can find the gift in it. Our culture certainly doesn't think of it that way; age is something to be stalled off as long as possible, just as we're supposed to be delighted that summer is hanging on into late September. Death is supposed to be something we fend off too, and we think we can do so, keeping our "quality of life" until we conveniently die in our sleep, in perfect mental and physical condition at the age of ninety-eight. We forget, as usual, that biology is one of the three jokers in the deck (the other two, as I've said elsewhere, being physics and human free will).

But I've found in the past that there are great gifts in the desert, and fruit and fresh water in what look like desolate places, once we accept the necessity of being in them for a while. Adversity has a habit of stripping down life, and properly considered this may be a blessing. Perhaps in aging, I may lose what sense I have left that I'm in control of things and learn a bit more humility; perhaps I'll learn to look for the same good things that I see, when I search for them, in the quiet grays and browns of mud season.

Or maybe—who knows?—I'll learn something completely different. I've never really considered the possibility that I might age into scarlets and oranges and indecently brilliant purples, flourishing greens and knock-your-eye-out peacock blue. Maybe, after a life largely spent in being responsible, obedient, caretaking, perfectionistic—after having spent far too much time trying to be drably good and not even trying to dance—I'll turn into a truly wicked old woman, a biker-chick granny. There may be hope for me yet.

But whatever happens, I know that between now and then my job has to be to braid my soul so tightly that when my mind starts to age, and all my pretenses and defenses fall away as the leaves drop from the trees, what's honestly left is something approaching a grownup and a Christian. I may not succeed: that joker biology, after all. But I can try.

I know that as my personal end-of-summer approaches, the time has come for me to set out on another journey, one not so much away from the God of my parents, my church, and my tradition as toward a God who is bigger and more mysterious, but who is also specially and particularly *mine*. It's not what I'd choose; at my age, I'd rather stay at home in tolerable comfort. But the second journey seems to be in the course of choosing me. I know from way back that when it feels as though we aren't given choices, sometimes it's because God is only asking us to go along with what He has in mind. I have found that the only sensible answer under these circumstances is, "OK, Lord, whatever."

Well, Lord, OK. Whatever. I'll still choose you, knowing that the choice is a fresh one, made every day. I'll still choose you even if it means mud season instead of a glorious autumn. This time, though, it's not going to be force of habit, or something I do for someone else; this time, I have to choose you in complete freedom, knowing that this choice will take me into my own autumn, my own winter (however long it lasts) and beyond.

Shall we get on with it, Lord? Just let me know where we're going. Or (on second thought) no, don't: you never have in the past, and why should *everything* change?

Jenny Jemima

I buried her in the old flower garden, with a big rock for her headstone, next to the white lilac. My two sons, whose lives she had graced for fourteen years, dug the hole. It didn't have to be very big; by the time she died, she weighed so little, six pounds and a bit. When, at the vet's office, I shrouded her small body in a fresh white towel, I tucked her into her favorite sleeping position, curled up tight, chin on paws, tail neatly draped over her nose. I stroked her fur, still silky but neglected while she was too ill to groom. Then I tucked the sides and ends of the towel around her and pinned them into place. She made a small but surprisingly weighty package. When I transferred her from the cardboard box in which

I'd brought her home into the hole in the garden, I dropped some wild violets on the towel. I should have said something, some prayers, some words in memory; but it didn't occur to me. You have to be young to think of having a funeral for a cat. I was too busy trying to get through it all without falling apart.

We'd had her since she was an eight-week-old kitten, and she was, of all the cats I've coexisted with, easily the sweetest-natured and most loving. Not that she couldn't be a spitfire: she played a demon game of boogeties through the upstairs banisters, and she could swear like a trooper at the other cats if they bugged her. (Boogeties, for you non-cat people, is the game of running your fingers along the banister uprights as you stand on the stairs, in order to get a lurking cat to attack them.) But when a child, or an adult for that matter, was in tears or distress, she had a way of showing up, dancing up on her immaculate white paws, rubbing up against you sweetly to bring comfort, calling out "Mrrf?" It is not normally in the job description of cats to be loving, but there are exceptions, and she was one.

We didn't know it was cancer until we took her to the vet; we knew only that she'd stopped eating, wasn't grooming in her usual hypermeticulous way, and was losing weight. She was so sad. The vet found the tumor in her mouth, a big one. Holding her two days later, as the sedative shot took effect and she stretched out in my arms, waiting for the second shot, the one that would stop her heart and her breathing, I could see properly, for the first time, how the cancer had eaten away at her lower lip. She must have been in pain, but she didn't say, except for a low growl once or twice when it must have been getting to her. Animals can't tell you. Sometimes you can't guess.

We had the standard discussion around her death: it is impossible to have known Jenny-cat without believing that she did indeed have a soul—a small-cat-sized soul, but definitely a soul. This may be theologically inaccurate, but who cares? Animals who are beloved and loving are different. Or maybe our Aboriginal brethren and sistren have it right and *all* animals have souls, are valued individuals in the eye of the Creator; I wouldn't argue with that.

Who are we, we sinners, to claim that because we have language and build houses, we get a monopoly on this soul business? That's just another way of our setting ourselves apart from creation, seeing ourselves as superior—and look where *that's* gotten us. Maybe it is the purpose of dolphinhood to be as dolphinish as possible, and dolphins who do this are a delight to God, and maybe the same is true of bedbugs or tilapia fish, or even (shudder!) zebra mussels (although not in the wrong places). We may be little below the angels, but given how unlike angels we behave wouldn't God want a little tender, or comic, relief from us sometimes? Isn't all beauty a comment on God's giftedness in creation, and isn't this as true for the silk of a cat's soft back as it is of a sunset or Bach's *Mass in B Minor*?

Of one thing, however, I am quite sure: God has his fingers and senses skimming through the universe of his own making, like any other artist, looking for whatever good can be scooped out and put to useful account. I think of my friend Martine, the artist, and her tableful of odds and ends, waiting to be put to creative use in glasswork or enameling. I think of my friend Anne, the writer, storing snippets of village gossip and supermarket conversations, nipping them out of the small-town puddle, stowing them in memory and waiting to put them to use. I trail my own fingers through life, seeing what might be useful. That's what creativity is all about.

I think of God trolling through creation, looking for the good bits, something to create with; and I see this tiny cat-sized soul, this beloved and loving furperson, slipping into God's hand and probably purring quite loudly. I can't see God passing up a bit of love just because it animated a mere domestic shorthair, not a person, not when God needs all the bits of love that are out there. Then God, having delightedly received this furperson, would figure out where to bestow her. He would know what she could become: a grandeur of gentleness, a bit of peace widening gyrelike to absorb and obliterate hurt and disorder. Something along those lines. The fur of her breast would shine white as a new star, clean as she always kept it, until her illness took her.

Love is love, is love, is love. Surely the human soul is capable of whole prodigies of love, but I've seen, God help me, too much evidence of the opposite. Humans sometimes seem to be in full flight from love, bolting toward selfishness and self-justification and self-righteousness, vices that a cat would never even consider. Yes, we have more capacity for love than cats do. But Jenny's tiny feline capacity for love was further developed than so many human beings' far greater capacity to love. Which pleases God more greatly: a sprig of catnip that grows and becomes all the catnip it can be, or an acorn that just sits there and says "I don't have time for all this dumb oak-tree-growing stuff"?

My Jenny, God's critter (as am I), died in my arms on a Wednesday morning. Now she lies out under the white lilac, and I don't like to think what will, in the days and weeks to come, happen to her silky, beautifully clean coat and her huge shining eyes. This is part of the nature of things, but a part one doesn't like to think of for a person (skin or fur) that one's known so nearly, and loved. There won't be a familiar, apparently boneless presence on my bed again. Jenny-cat, who I took as a kitten from the animal shelter and who was part of my life for fourteen years, is dead. I know; I held her as she died.

I trust that God receives Jenny-cat in ways that I cannot begin to ask or imagine but will learn about in the fullness of God's time, *kairos,* when I walk along the banks of that River. Maybe a small, beautifully groomed black-and-white tabby cat will emerge from the bushes, trotting up on tiny spotless paws with tail firmly erect, and writhe around my ankles, giving me The Look: "Mrrf. I've been waiting. What kept you?"

❧ Billy Bly ☙

I haven't talked to Billy in ages, but I always enjoyed our conversations. Intellectually, they weren't stimulating—we just cooed at each other—but Billy's cooing made a mourning dove sound like a rooster.

Billy's birth went very, very badly. His spinal column got driven up into the base of his brain, leaving him alive but profoundly brain-damaged. He's in his twenties now. He has significant physical problems and virtually no intellectual capacity. He can respond to love, especially to loving touch. He can respond to sound and makes plenty of sound himself. He identifies his beloved stepmother, my near-sister Deb, as "Diih." He comes home to visit his Diih and his father Bill, and the three of them cuddle and play and have a lovely time, but his needs are too great and too constant, and once he got big Deb and Bill couldn't manage any more. Billy spends most of his days in a (very good) institution for the profoundly damaged.

When I think of Billy, I have a very hard time with the notion that somehow when we die we vanish as individuals into the great Oneness. Billy has never had, and never will have in this life, the chance to individuate, to flourish, or not in any way that we can understand. Those who know him believe that at a deep spiritual level Billy *does* flourish, but this doesn't alter the fact that, although he may have experiences the "well" among us will never have, he will necessarily miss out on most of what this world offers human beings. Social justice can do little for Billy except ensure his physical comfort and his respectful treatment—no minor thing. But there's nothing we can do to set Billy to rights in this life.

I can get around this for my own soul's comfort by envisaging a life to come in which Billy *can* be fully healed—can own and exercise to their fullest the gifts that should have been his if his birth hadn't gone so badly awry. In such a world I can imagine all that's best about Billy—his sweetness, his very real spirituality, his connection with God—developing in a relation of deepest, most childlike trust, which is the best of his life in this world. But I can also imagine his delight at learning (if not as we do in this life, as children, though in some other equally real way) how to hold things, how to see with clarity, how to move purposefully, to walk, to run, to make love, to hold his own child—all the things that give beauty to our lives in this world. I can imagine him finally being free of the physical pain he suffers from joints and tendons that seize up because he can't work them. I can imagine him leaping with the joyous arrogance of the young.

Then I think about all the other damaged souls. Billy's damage is large and obvious, but what of the people I see downtown? The parolees from federal prisons? The families of those still behind bars? The hundreds of mentally ill people who have been ejected from the psychiatric hospital because of budget cuts? This city is full of the poor, the screwed-up, the obviously troubled. You can get used to it; in fact, you have to. But I can't see their faces without seeing the sharp marks of deep damage or (even worse) the deadened look that children take on when they've been abused.

I know too that I don't have to go down the socioeconomic ladder to find trouble; nobody living in this city can fail to be aware that there are walking wounded in the university community, among those who seem respectable and prosperous— and sometimes the wounds are worsened by being so carefully hidden ("we're not going to talk about that"). I could find children of respectable families whose needs went unmet in subtle ways that sometimes leave more damage than do more obvious wounds.

Or I could just go to AA or Al-Anon or Narcotics Anonymous and look around the circle. This is a broken world, full of pain, and we seem to spend an inordinate amount of time trying to duck the fact.

I could look within myself, at what seems to be a pile of emotional baggage large enough to fill a Pullman car. I look at the childhood damage, the failed relationships, the careers that never got off the ground, love withheld out of fear and mistrust, a life I have not valued as I should. Oh yes, I need healing too.

I can't imagine a God so unjust as to deprive those whose lives have been so shortchanged in this world, by damage to body or mind, the fulfillment of *all* their promise. I also can't imagine a God who would want us to develop the fullness of our own souls in community with others and with God, and who would then not want to see those souls develop even further in richness, depth, and joy. When I die, I envision for my own soul a process of undoing all the wrong I have done and suffered—of being set finally and definitively to rights; and then a growing in glory and delight, at least until time ends and God's work reaches its full conclusion.

A person needs hope to keep going, especially when life turns tragic (by this world's judging, at least). I hope for Billy. I hope for all those who are damaged beyond repair in body or mind. I hope for myself. "We look for the resurrection of the body and the life of the world to come."

Knitters have an expression, "frogging," for ripping an in-progress piece off the needles and unraveling it back several rows or even inches in order to correct a mistake. You don't frog for trivial reasons, only for real booboos. But any experienced knitter knows that frogging is as essential to knitting as is the purl stitch. I would like to believe that in the life to come God frogs Billy Bly right back to the disaster of his birth and reknits him, through happy infancy and the period between mobility and discretion, through a real childhood and adolescence, into a rich and fulfilling life, so that Billy gets to experience everything life denied him. I'd like to hope that God does the same for me too, in all my far lesser (but still adequately grievous) bits of long-standing damage. I would like, please God, to be set truly to rights. As only God can do it.

❧ At the Dentist's ❧

I lie back in the chair, letting my mind amble off into a mild twirling-in-the-breeze meditative state. Over my head, the dentist and his assistant chat as he works away on a lower-left hind molar. He is very good with novocaine, and I have learned to ignore the drilling. I am oddly content.

I may be the only person of my acquaintance who'd rather see the dentist than the doctor. This sounds nuts, but I have my reasons.

My family physician (the only one I could get in with when I moved here) is a cardiologist at the university teaching hospital who also has a general practice. He is lean, Australian, authoritative, clipped in hair and manner, and very professional. His concern, obviously, is my physical health.

He terrifies me.

Dentists, I have found, are more easy-going and pragmatic. They've seen everything, after all, so the state of my teeth (not wonderful) is something they tend to be tolerant about. None of this "we're going to whip those choppers into shape and just think what a beautiful smile you'll have!"—at least not from my current dentist. It's more like: "These are the teeth God and your parents gave you, and you have not been perfect about caring for them, and we both know you don't have the sort of money you'd need to acquire that white-tombstone look, so let's do what we can with what we've got. Now, open wide. This won't hurt a bit."

This may be because dentists aren't ranked as high in the socioeconomic scheme of things and therefore have pleasantly modest egos. It may be because dentists are aware that one's teeth are only a part of one's physical being, and not a part that's apt to kill you if something goes wrong. My dentist is an artist, and it pleases him greatly to do his work well, but he doesn't have the single-minded clarity of vision that I've tended to find in physicians (not in all, by any means, but in many).

It's exactly this single-minded clarity of vision that daunts and defeats me. The vision is not my vision, but I don't know how even to open this particular conversation, much less how to get my point across.

How do I say to this doctor of mine—this man who fights passionately in the operating room to rescue the dying who desperately want to live—"I'm sorry, sir, but for some of us, death isn't the Great Enemy, but a friend and a sister who comes to take us home"?

Could he hear me? I don't know. I know I'm too afraid to speak the words.

We've come a long way from the old heresy that said soul is good and body is bad; we've come to understand that if it were true, God would never have done this incarnation bit. If God could see fit to inhabit human flesh, then flesh is good. True, this is not an observation widely made in post-Christian society, but some of us still believe it.

Going by the news and women's magazines in the doctor's waiting room (bursting, all of them, with advice on how to max out your lymph system or fine-tune your folic acid intake), I'd say we have erred in the equal and opposite direction. Flesh is good, but should flesh be God?

My physician could fault me for not giving adequate worthship to my long-term physical well-being. I do make some effort to behave in medically responsible ways, but not many. I'm just not into it. This puts me squarely out of whack with current cultural standards, which say that my aim should be to max out my life, both in years and quality. It becomes a long chess game played with every ounce of intelligence and determination and the will to win, with healthy living and medicine on one side and morbidity and mortality on the other.

But what if I don't want to play that game? What if I'm interested in something very different, something modern Western medicine rarely touches?

We knew once, but we have denied and forgotten, something fundamental: ultimately we all die. My friend Susan Urbach put it neatly: nobody gets off this planet alive. My death is part of my life, as necessary as my birth, and for me the two are alike—not a defeat by darkness, but a transit from darkness into greater light. Not an end, but a glorious beginning.

"You can't possibly know that," my doctor might say. How could I explain to him this deep gut-certainty that has nothing to do with stories of near-death-experiences and everything to do with the community of saints? It's a vision some of us share, quietly, with a word or two, not needing to say much because we're all aware of the same reality ("Yes, this is what it will taste like. This is what we have to look forward to"). For us, it's a deep truth that's on a skew line with biomedical factoids; it neither parallels them nor intersects them but operates in an entirely different plane.

Honest scientists say there are areas of truth that science has no truck with; it lacks the tools for the measurement of things that (science knows in its rational bones) are inherently immeasurable. With apologies to the many excellent physicians out there, I'm not sure how far Western medicine is honest science. It certainly isn't being honest whenever it denies the deep connection between body and spirit and the power of healthy spirituality. It isn't honest when it promises the trusting masses that healthy living will buy them radiant health into advanced old age. Western medicine isn't honest if it sets up health as a god and promises that worship of this deity will bring a long and happy life.

I don't long for death (although I did for a while, when life was too harsh to love). I want to see my kids fully established. I'd like to see what life has to offer for the next few years. But to see death as an enemy to be defeated at all costs? That's just plain folly.

> *Never weather-beaten sail*
> *More willing bent to shore;*
> *Never tired pilgrim's limbs*
> *Affected slumber more*
> *Than my weary sprite now longs*
> *To fly out of my troubled breast:*
> *O come quickly, sweetest Lord,*
> *And take my sprite to rest.*
> —THOMAS CAMPION

CHAPTER 8

God-Stuff

For God alone my soul waits
in silence;
from him comes my salvation.
He alone is my rock and my
salvation,
my fortress; I shall never be
shaken.

—PSALM 62:1–2

✣ Of Ropes and Cooties ✣

From there he set out and went away to the region of Tyre. He entered a house and did not want anyone to know he was there. Yet he could not escape notice, but a woman whose little daughter had an unclean spirit immediately heard about him, and she came and bowed down at his feet. Now the woman was a Gentile, [a Greek] of Syrophoenician origin. She begged him to cast the demon out of her daughter. He said to her, "Let the children be fed first, for it is not fair to take the children's food and throw it to the dogs." But she answered him, "Sir, even the dogs under the table eat the children's crumbs." Then he said to her, "For saying that, you may go—the demon has left your daughter." So she went home, found the child lying on the bed, and the demon gone. [MARK 7:24–30]

Before we get going with this particular chunk of Gospel, I'd like to introduce an important theological term. Don't worry; it has only two syllables, and it doesn't come from Greek.

The term is "cooties."

For those of you who have forgotten elementary school, *cooties* describes a sort of invisible but contagious nonbiological germ. Cooties don't make you sick; they make you *icky*. If you haven't encountered the concept, just think how a ten-year-old boy reacts to being kissed by a girl. Girl germs! Grossout! Yuck!

Definitions done, let's get back to the Gospel. Context, first: this passage comes right after a passage in which Jesus has been tearing up one side of the Pharisees and down the other for worshiping technical correctness more than God. He says that what matters isn't precise obedience to the rules, but what comes from the heart.

So now we get a quick change of scene. Jesus has gone off to what's now Lebanon, clear out of Israel. As always, word of his healing power gets out. This time he's among a mixed population: Jews, Greeks, Phoenicians, Canaanites—the people of modern Palestine.

Now, these Gentiles are, by Jesus' own cultural standards, badly afflicted with cooties, or (to invent a word that the English language sorely needs) they are *cootified*. They don't, of course, keep the Mosaic Law, but even if they tried, it wouldn't matter. They still wouldn't be Jews. You could be Jewish only by being born to a Jewish mother. The law puts a barrier—think of it as a sort of dividing rope, like the ropes they use to organize bank lines—between Gentile and Jew, to keep the Jews cootie-free.

That wasn't the only rope. There were ropes separating men from women. Outside the house, a good Jewish man would no more speak to a woman than he would eat pork. She might be menstruating, and that would give her cooties, and she'd give them to anyone who touched her. Men wouldn't take the risk.

On with the story: this Gentile woman has a sick little girl—most likely with some neurological or behavioral disorder, epilepsy or severe autism, perhaps. The woman has heard that Jesus is a healer. So she approaches him, looking for help.

Sounds perfectly reasonable, no? But to Jesus? He's a man. He's a Jew. She's a Gentile; she's a woman. She has cooties on her cooties. It wouldn't matter if she kept a kosher kitchen and lived a perfectly virtuous life. She's wrong, not for anything she's done but for who she *is*. There's nothing she could ever do to change that.

But she's scared for her kid and she's going to get his help, and she doesn't care what she has to do to get it. So she calls out, "Lord, please heal my daughter!"

Our loving Lord—our tender, loving, gentle shepherd who suffers little children to come to him—what does he do?

He turns into a Pharisee. He does exactly the sort of thing that was driving him nuts when the Pharisees did it a short while ago. "What I've got is for the children, not the dogs," he says. "Scram. Beat it. You're icky. Take a hike." I'd like to think that he answers this way because he's too tired and strung-out to think straight; but to the woman, it's still a slap in the face. "Dog" is a *really* vile term in that part of the world.

But she's desperate and determined, and her child's life is at stake. Also, she *believes* in him, really believes. Quick-witted, she fields his response, gives it a twist, and fires it back at him like a fastball: "Maybe we're dogs, but I'll settle for crumbs."

There are those who hold that Jesus' initial response is just a sort of tease, a test that the woman managed to pass. This bothers me, since I prefer to believe in a God who does not mess around with people's minds. That's why I prefer another way of looking at the scene. Maybe my way is wrong, but it's interesting.

I'd like to think that she manages to look right at him as she speaks, although she probably doesn't. I'd like to think that suddenly he *sees* her as a warm, living, loving human being instead of a foreign female thing with cooties.

I'd like to think that he suddenly sees how his own cultural righteousness has turned him into exactly the sort of person he just railed against. I'd like to think that he is, for a moment, appalled by his own reaction. These words that come out of his mouth: what do they say about what's in *his* heart?

I'd like to think that in the breaking moment, seeing her hurt, her humanity, her desperation, her love for her child, he hits the wall. Since she cannot change who she is, he has to change what he thinks. "Thou shalt love thy neighbor as thyself."

I would like to think that in this moment he hears the quiet voice, his Abba's voice, deep in his soul: "Child, child, hear Me: Love trumps the Law. Always."

I believe that, in this moment, Jesus changes profoundly.

Whatever goes on in his mind, his action is clear. He reaches right over the rope that stands between them, and he does the right and needful thing: "For saying that, you may go. The demon has left your daughter."

It's a fine story, a remarkable story. But what does it say to us?

We've been doing it for years, we Christians, along with everybody else: we've set up a rope to divide the pure guys from the icky people, the people with cooties.

The early church struggled with the issue of including Gentiles; it was a huge battle. Eventually, thanks largely to Paul, the church moved the rope and included Gentiles. And lo! the Gentiles had no cooties.

Sadly, the church then included women *out.* For most of two millennia, Christianity taught "the daughters of Eve" that they were inherently flawed by the fact of being female. It held that having two X chromosomes gives you cooties. We only started to move the rope about thirty-five years ago. And lo! whatever nine-year-old boys may think, girls don't have cooties.

The church supported society's choice to put a rope between white people and people of color, until only about forty-five years ago. We enslaved and exploited these people, quoting the Bible freely, until finally, ordinary civil justice smacked us hard upside the head and yelled "Stop it!" Slowly, too slowly, we've moved the rope. And lo! persons of color don't have cooties.

Here in Canada we put our Native peoples—those who welcomed us to these shores in the first place—on the wrong side of the rope, and we thought we were doing them a real favor by teaching them to be non-Native, beating their very identity out of them in residential schools. Too many of them, and too many white Canadians, still believe they have cooties. But trust me, Aboriginal people are cootie-free.

We still put the poor on the wrong side of the rope. They're wimps, they're losers, they don't try hard enough. They're icky. Oh, they believe us—just walk down Princess Street, our main drag, where the panhandlers hang out, and you'll see it in their eyes. Do they really have cooties? Not one bit.

All along, whenever we've stretched a rope dividing right people from wrong people, whenever we've shouted "Eeew!" at some of God's children, we've *always* cited selected (very selected) passages of Scripture to justify our position. We give certain texts extra importance while dismissing texts that don't matter so much. We *all*, without exception, pick and choose from Scripture. We no longer seek to stone to death brides who are found to be nonvirgins, at least not in these parts. We don't hand along widowed sisters-in-law to the next brother down, to perpetuate the line. So much for meticulously observing God's rules about sex.

Now we're caught up in a new rope-and-cooties issue. We're fighting about whether homosexuality is a normal part of human existence or a wrong way of being. Regardless of how faithful, loving, mature, responsible, and soul-nourishing they are, we say that *all* homosexual relationships are still wrong. We call homosexuality "a lifestyle choice," and we call it sinful by its very nature. Our judgment of our same-sex siblings hurts and angers them, because we aren't *listening* to them. We've dismissed them, just as Jesus dismissed the woman in Tyre. We offer them only two choices: to betray their own souls by faking being straight, or to live in lifelong involuntary celibacy. Anything else, we say, is sin.

Homosexual people tell us that their sexual orientation is not something they've opted into; it's part of their being. Like the Syrophoenician woman, they can't change who they are.

We, on the other hand, can change what we believe.

If we're at all honest with ourselves, we've done this before, lots of times. Mostly, we've changed in the direction of being more inclusive, more liberating. Look at our stance on divorce, for example, or contraception.

But it hasn't been a stampede toward "anything goes"—not by any means. We no longer accept marital rape or spousal abuse. We have begun to understand that sexual abuse of children is devastating, although we're still just beginning to understand the implications and take a serious stand against child pornography, which requires the violation of living victims. We adhere to the Geneva Conventions. We prosecute hate crimes. We've rejected slavery; we protest against abuses of human rights. We preach—even if we don't always practice—respect for all human souls. We see war as an evil thing. These too are un-Biblical (at least if we stick to the Old Testament).

So it's not a matter of uncritically accepting everything the culture hands us. What we're doing, instead, is discernment—holding what we learn from this world in one hand, and God's self-revelation in the other, and thoughtfully considering how to bring them together in the Kingdom way.

Our discernment tries to figure out the Will of God, the Mind of Christ. Yes, Jesus confronts sins (although somehow it doesn't occur to us to confront the same sins that Jesus confronts, such as hypocrisy and greed). But who does Jesus put his arms around? The excluded, the unwelcome, those on the wrong side of the rope—even those icky cootified Samaritans!

More than that, far more than that: God Himself ducks under the thick dividing rope and comes over to stand among us—for we *all* have cooties, and God knows that, and strangely, it doesn't seem to make Her love us one bit less.

I want to stand on the same side of the rope as the poor and the oppressed and the other cootified sinners, for this is where I find my brother Jesus. You may find him somewhere else, of course; I'm not prescribing for you, and I respect our differences. For me, though, I'd still rather take a risk for love, because that's what Jesus did for me.

I believe with all my heart that our Lord got it right, so long ago in Tyre, holding his suffering sister in one hand, and his own legalism and unthinking prejudice in the other, and saying to himself, "I've got to make a choice here,"—and then choosing her, cooties and all. Because that's where the life was.

"Child, child, Love trumps the Law," Abba-God whispers deep in our souls.

"Always. You hear Me?"

⚜ The Bee ⚜

I heard it as I was going up the stairs with a basket of clean laundry: a deep, frantic buzzing. It sounded almost like a drill. Too loud to be even the biggest housefly, too deep and grumbly to be a hornet; must be a bee. I set the basket down and went back downstairs again, looking for a plastic cup and a slip of cardboard and swearing to myself. Dishes to do, supper to start, shopping to take care of, bee to deal with—dammit, no wonder I never seem to get any real work done.

This household has a defined policy for members of the phyllum Arthropoda (what most people call "bugs," although it also includes crustaceans). We are not fond of the Diptera prevalent around here, mostly flies and mosquitoes, which are slapped or swatted when caught. Although we don't kill them, we are also not partial to the Dermaptera (earwigs), for no very good reason except that they're so yucky-looking. Lepidoptera (moths, mostly) we simply live with; likewise Coleoptera (beetles), although we're extremely fond of ladybugs. The Odonata (dragonflies) never come in, but we love them dearly; not only are they fascinating and gorgeous in their own right but they munch the dipterids that munch on us. As for the class Arachnida (spiders), they are honored guests; we are highly web-friendly. For much of last fall and winter, we cherished a particularly handsome specimen named Bubbles, until (s)he vanished into the pantry, never to be seen again. Finally, let's leave centipedes, mites, and fleas out of this. (Author's note: for this paragraph, I hit up the online Encyclopedia Britannica and checked with our local naturalists. I'm really hopelessly ignorant; I just have good sources.)

But what about the Hymenoptera, the hive-dwellers, the swarmers, including the girls with the stingers in their butts? They are a tad more problematic. Wasps and hornets we kill—not happily, but we are too afraid of them to trap and release them. Ants get in the food, which we don't like, and my elder son detests them, so they too get the boot. Bees, on the other hand, get rescued and put outside. Which is why I went downstairs looking for cup and cardboard.

It was a honeybee, I think—certainly not one of the huge, fat, fuzzy bumblers, but something sleeker and more dangerous-looking. She was throwing herself against the glass of the upstairs hall window, trying to get out.

I waited until she'd settled down, buzzing frantically against one spot on the windowpane; then I trapped her by carefully putting the cup mouth over her and against the glass, sliding the bit of cardboard under to hold her in. Her buzz went from deep growl to hysterical scream, like an engine being gunned, as I carried her down the front stairs; this was one *really* upset bee-person. Fortunately, the front door was wide open; I kicked the screen door, took the bee out on the front porch, pointed the cup at the front yard, and let her fly.

It occurred to me, as I got into the dishes, how much like salvation this whole thing is. There we are, trapped, seeing where we should be, where we really belong, but kept from it by something we can't really see and certainly can't get through. We panic as the bee panicked, buzzing against this strange barrier; our efforts are furious and futile, but we don't seem to understand that we cannot break through, not without help. The strange thing is that so often we need to be even *further* trapped—caught in a mystifying, maybe terrifying place that we think is leading to death—before we can be set free.

The important thing about salvation is that it catches us where we're trapped and it frees us when we cannot free ourselves. Just as the bee had done nothing to deserve its own freedom, so we do nothing to deserve ours. It's all done out of God's sheer, generous love.

God's cup-and-cardboard act is, however, nothing like mine; there's nothing so crudely mechanical about how we get rescued. He may, for example, work through the love of those around us or the kindness of strangers. God finds ways of working in our lives that are highly creative and sometimes a little weird. Or the saving process may be so subtle that we have no idea what's going on, any more than the bee knew what I was going to do with her. Her rescue was (from her perspective) dramatic, terrifying, even traumatic, and sometimes that's what we experience with God. But our rescue often comes more gently, even imperceptibly. What it always involves, though, is turning away from the false way out— from pounding against a wall we can't see but that blocks us from real life—to true liberation.

We may never fully realize or understand what it is that set us free. God is too big and we are too small and limited to be able to understand all that God's about.

Have I been saved? You betcha: saved from certain death by beating myself up against what looked like the light and what was, in fact, a hard, defeating surface. I knew at the time that salvation was at work, but it was not an easy or pretty process, and I'm not sure it's finished yet. Salvation isn't necessarily a once-and-always affair. At least not in my experience.

Drying the plates, I thought: the bee took off from the cup as though she had been fired from a gun, shooting off into a perfect May afternoon, rejoicing (in her apian way) in being free once again in a world full of flowering. I think I remember a bit of how that felt. I hope she found her way home.

☙ The Poster ❧

It was one of those afternoons. I was anxious to get a poster mailed off. The last mail truck pick-up in town is 4:30. The poster mailer I needed to mail the thing was available at the stationery store that also has a postal outlet. So I got together poster and slip of paper with the mailing address it was going to, parka, boots, gloves (it's cold out), glasses, purse . . . purse? Purse? Not in the house. Not in my car. Where's my purse?

Oops.

I knew, with the utter certainty that a woman has about her purse (part of a strange but extremely close relationship—guys, don't even try to understand this), exactly where my purse was. It was at a friend's house in Bishop's Mills, where I'd gone earlier in the afternoon to pick up the poster. Bishop's Mills is about twenty minutes southwest of here.

I could just do it.

In these parts, driving southwest at fourish on a clear January afternoon means you are driving straight into the sun, and the sun's position is at an angle well below your car's sun visor. The air is so dry and clear that the sun is very, very bright. Oh, what fun. If you have no sunglasses, the best you can do is squint and hold up a gloved hand, trying to block the sun itself without losing too much view of the road. I thought how little I really like looking at the sun, or even being in extremely bright light. If God is like the sun, as so many hymns and visionaries say, I'm in real trouble.

At the train crossing on Route 18, the pole was down and the lights were flashing. Train crossing. Oh. I see. They've been delivering the new year–model cars to the city. They expect to sell a lot of cars, evidently, given the number of empty car-carrier railway cars. Long wait. Train vanishes; pole rises; once again I'm driving into the sunset.

Got to Bishop's Mills. Found purse at friend's house. Headed back to town, this time with the sun (thank God!) behind me. What I do like is the way the slanting light glorifies things, giving the poor broken woods a living lightness, turning a stand of plumed grass to softly glowing gold.

Back along Highway 18, and at the level crossing the pole was down *again,* dammit. This *never* happens, two trains within ten minutes of each other. This train was heading into the city with a load of late-model cars. Boy, they really are optimistic about car sales. This time I was lead car in the line, and I got to see the three diesel engines thundering by, and I thought: I find this mightiness and power rather scary. If God is might and power, how am I going to cope with him?

If God is brighter than a thousand suns, I cannot imagine spending eternity staring at him in worshipful adoration. Maybe that's how it will be; I just can't fancy it from where I am now. If God is might and power, am I going to find him formidable and overwhelming? These may be real and important aspects of God, but I find them more off-putting than attractive.

I know what I want in a God: I want a God who is gentle and tender and careful in handling people's bruised souls. I want a God of quiet green spaces with a great silver river flowing through, a God of delightful company and the sweetest music. I also want a God of deep-shadowed mountain woods, full of dancing mischief and Dionysian giggles. I want a God of silver fish leaping, and the curl of a new fern, and the fractal of the edge of the tide moving in. I want a God of joy; I'm just not quite sure what joy will taste like.

But if there's anything at all I know, it's that I don't get to choose what God is like. I cannot specify a Deity who is all mercy, nor one who is all judgment and stern righteousness. I cannot limit God to any form or aspect, however fetching I might personally find the version or how it suits my own so-limited vision. God is God is God, and I don't get to write the specifications.

But perhaps God, in God's great kindness, chooses (in dealing with any one of us, in our mortality and human frailty) to match God's self to whatever we can manage to accept. I can't look into the sun without doing real and permanent damage to my sight; that's asking too much of my retinas. I can't hold out my arms to three thundering Canadian National diesel engines, asking for an embrace; if I try that, I will be hamburger on the tracks, and that's terribly upsetting to the poor engineers, not to mention my near and dear ones.

But if, given what life's been like, I want and desperately need a God who's like a big fuzzy fleece that I can drive my fingers into and press my face up against, for comfort and a safe place to cry, then maybe—just maybe—God's willing to be like that for my sake, until I'm ready for something better and bigger.

What I must never do is say that God *is* the big fuzzy fleece. This is a form of idolatry. God is infinitely bigger than that, and infinitely more mysterious. I doubt I will ever, in no matter how many thousand ages in the life to come, be able to walk all the way around God, much less comprehend God's totality. There will always be more of God than I can ask or imagine, and that's the mystery.

Moving a blue streak, I got to the stationery store and postal outlet—and found that the mail had already been picked up. Got poster mailer. Sped downtown to the main post office, where I still had a few minutes before the truck left. Got to counter of main post office . . . and realized I had left the bit of paper with the mailing address at the stationery store.

Oh well. It'll have to wait till Monday.

❧ The Water Is Wide ❧

I swear to God, sometimes God has to spend more effort and energy breaking my grip on things than any reasonable deity should have to.

When we were still hip-deep in renovations to the new house, one bit of drywall mudding wasn't going well. It was in the front hall, right next to the door into what was to be the kitchen—a very public place indeed. But there was a bump in the drywall that I couldn't get rid of. Didn't matter how many coats of drywall compound I put on, how carefully I feathered the edges, how meticulously I sanded, the bump was still there.

Struggling with this, one Tuesday morning, I realized something basic: for all the apparent differences, drywall mudding is essentially the same activity as frosting a cake. I was always terrible at cake frosting. This doesn't greatly bother me because in the grand scheme of things, a neatly frosted cake is not high on my list of things that matter. Drywall mudding, on the other hand, is permanent and visible, and if it looks terrible, I'm going to have to live with it for as long as I own this house. So I put on another coat, despairing, and waited.

Wednesday morning: hit the bump once again with the sander—and sanding drywall is, most renovators would agree, a disgusting activity. It's incredibly messy. It generates huge amounts of fine white dust that gets into, onto, under, and through absolutely everything. Drywall dust got up my nose and settled in my hair, making it feel like dirty sheep's wool.

Sanding didn't make the bump go away. However I struggled with it, it was having nothing of this flat-wall business. It had decided otherwise. That, the bump said, is that. This was the point at which, totally defeated and fed to the hind teeth with four months of moving and renovations, I burst into tears and fled the house.

For reasons I did not stop to analyze, I found myself making a mad dash downtown for the ferry that crosses over the harbor to Wolfe Island. A ferry ride, I felt, would do me good.

I was right. Simply being on the ferry stopped the voice of panicky, doom-ridden overresponsibility that tends to chitter away like a demented squirrel in my head. I left my car and sat on the upper deck, looking out over the water, taking in the quiet thrumming roar of the great engines, the smell of fresh marine paint and diesel fuel. Spread out before me, the water lay gray and sparkling; the spring wind, sharp as a loving tap, blew the drywall dust off me, out of my hair, out of my soul.

Child.

That voice I hadn't heard in such a long time.

Child.

Abba?

Child.

'S that you?

You know who I am.

Oh, Abba. It's been so long.

We talked silently all the way across the water, the voice and I. Anyone looking on would have seen only a tired middle-aged woman in a blue coat with white dust marks, looking quietly over the water. But inwardly, oh, we were busy, like old lovers, deprived of each other for far too long, touching, exploring, reassuring. *I am real. You are mine. You are loved.*

The water's not all that wide; the ferry ride takes only about half an hour. But on the water, time stretches—not the slumping, discouraged oh-god-when-will-this-end sag time goes into when life is being like that, but an expansion into eternity "like gold to airy thinness beat," as John Donne put it. I remembered what C. S. Lewis wrote in *The Screwtape Letters:* God wants us to live not in the past (with its memories of all that's gone wrong) or in the future (the fear that the future will only continue the past) but in the present, in this moment, for this is where our time is most like God's time—where *chronos* approaches *kairos,* just as, out on the lake past all the islands, the sky approaches the water with only the faintest line of horizon between the two.

Wolfe Island was lovely, a low, peaceable place of old plain farmhouses and rolled haybales and calm-faced shorthorns—no great shakes, if you're looking for natural beauty or tourist attractions, but a deeply friendly place. I ate a lunch of terrible meatloaf and real mashed potatoes at a placid old-fashioned restaurant. Then I drove out to the easternmost tip and watched a freighter glide gracefully along the shipping channel, heading for the St. Lawrence. Here, ship: I tossed my squirrelly anxieties and overre-sponsibility onto its deck. You take these away for me. You can dump them overboard when you reach the Gulf of St. Lawrence. They won't foul the water. They only foul my soul. For all shall be well and all shall be well and all manner of things shall be well.

I thought, on the ferry coming back: the more I fret and fume and grab onto responsibilities that I could in fact quite eas-ily shed, the more I distance myself from the voice. The more I fret about getting things just right, the more I slide into a deeper wrongness. The more I indulge the chittery-squirrel voice in my head, the less able I am to hear God's deep, calm tones. I have found myself, yet again, chasing around in ever-diminishing cir-cles until I have practically tried to climb my own back—and why?

To save a couple hundred dollars? Because I think I *should* be able to do everything perfectly? No, it's because I don't really trust anyone else to get the work done on time, I suppose. But according to whose schedule? Mine. Mine.

Dumb as a sack of hammers.

Back at the house, the bump on the wall looked a little less horrible. I resolved to find myself someone else to fix it; the hell with doing it myself. I felt something lighten and untwist.

About time, child.

That was Wednesday. On Thursday the electricians came. In order to fish wire from point A to point B, they had to punch four good-sized holes, right through the wall-bump, through all my anguished mudding.

Oh well.

The ferry runs back and forth several times a day, every day. I can always go back, any time I like.

⚜ Kyrie Eleison ⚜

At first hearing, it sounds like such a grovel: "Kyrie eleison" ("Lord, have mercy"). I *mean*. Talk about all the useless crud we've learned to discard: aristocracy, for example. Even in England, *Lord* doesn't have the same respect it used to. There's that patriarchal implication as well, the implicit dismissal of the feminine, especially in the longer classic version, the ancient Jesus prayer: "Lord Jesus Christ, only son of the Father, have mercy on me, a sinner": does it get more top-down, guilt-ridden, patriarchal-exclusive than that? And that's just the "Lord" part.

What about the "have mercy" part? Doesn't it imply a vindictive-bastard God, a God to whom we have to plead not to squish us like a bug? Haven't we finally gotten rid of the notion that we're all evil by birth, all the useless, crushing burden of guilt undeserved? Why on earth do we *need* mercy? And just what is mercy, anyway?

About the only word in "Lord, have mercy" that a person couldn't quarrel with is "have." That's because it's so completely neutral there's not much there to quarrel with.

So why, then, when my fingers close on the beads of my prayer chain, do I pray "Lord, have mercy"? I don't think I'm a fool; I know I'm not weak. I don't buy the old white-bearded vindictive-bastard God. I think rather highly of my very feminine ovaries—after all, they produced two gorgeous children. If someone attempts to pull rank on me, I'm apt to reach for a spitball with a certain determined gleam in my eye.

This bothered me enough that I went about the house for several days picking up things and putting them down again, forgetting where I left my glasses and hunting futilely for odd books and car keys. What *is* it about "Lord, have mercy"?

"Kyrie eleison": the prayer is incredibly ancient. It goes right back to the very beginning, so old that it stayed in Greek when the rest of the Mass was in Latin—so old that when we Anglicans dropped Latin for English, a lot of us kept "Kyrie eleison" around instead of saying the translation. It may be the best-known bit of Greek in Western civilization, now that I think of it: "Kyrie eleison, Christe eleison, Kyrie eleison" (Lord, have mercy; Christ, have mercy; Lord, have mercy). One for each member of the Trinity.

It is, you see, the chameleon of prayers, the prayer that can be so many things, shifting like the sheen on taffeta, like the colors of a gas slick. "Lord, have mercy": when I'm sick of myself, it's a prayer to free myself of me. When the world is being like that, it's not a prayer for protection. I do not pray that Daddy will shelter me from the storm or make it all better, because I have learned over time that Daddy does not work like that. Instead, it's a prayer for God's sustaining companionship. Whenever the pain or fear gets so bad I don't think I can breathe any more, or at least not nearly enough, it becomes a breathing prayer: inhale, exhale, "Lord, have mercy." It's a shape shifter, this prayer.

But it is a *prayer*. Relativism goes only so far before it gets ridiculous; "Lord, have mercy" cannot under any circumstances be said to mean "half a pound of onions" or "a lovely bunch of little pink daisies." It *does* say that God is much bigger than we are. It *does* say that God has the quality of mercy, and that we can evoke this mercy. It does acknowledge the otherness of God. The name for this otherness is *transcendence*; it says God spans all time, all space, unimaginably—while, at the same time, God inhabits us as the still small voice, small as a mustard seed, the immanent God.

I have a deep, long-standing love for the Kyrie from Bach's *Mass in B Minor*. It starts with three huge, forceful statements, battering rams at Heaven's gate, and then heads into a quiet juggernaut of a fugue, building into greater and greater force. The parts mount on top of each other, building up Godward, while the instrumental voices twine in an intricate sweetness that pierces heart and mind together. It's put together like a very fine old watch, and it shows such mastery as must make God the musician smile. I find when I try to listen to it that I can't track all the parts; if I manage to hold the voice lines together, I've mislaid the oboes or the burly basses. *But.* Although it's huge and intricate, it is also the most intimate music I can imagine, warm and rich with meaning and deep emotion; touches of sternness, yes; demanding; difficult; inexorable—but weaving back and forth into such tender searching as a lover might show, exploring his best-beloved for the very first time. Bach has his heart right out there in this piece, with all its splendid formality, and his heart is opened to God. It always is, after all. The piece ends in a burst of hope.

That's the paradox at the heart of the Kyrie: it is ancient and splendid, formal and respectful, and also so nakedly intimate. Lord, have mercy. Here I am before you, with no clothes on, so much smaller than you are, so vulnerable and fragile; please look on me with love, my dear.

I have another meaning for "Lord, have mercy," one that comes to me when I'm fingering my prayer beads, especially late at night when I'm tired and on the verge of falling asleep. A man I once knew told me that when his younger daughter was tiny, she used to crawl up onto his lap, tug at his wrist with her imperious starfish hand and say, in that won't-take-no-for-an-answer voice, "Arm *around!*" Meaning, "Put your arm around me, Daddy."

Lord, have mercy. Arm *around.* Thank you, Lord. That's right.

✿ Christe Eleison ✿

A few years back, the newspaper carried a story about an anthropologist in Israel who, using a skull of the right period, age, gender, and place, reconstructed what Jesus might have really looked like. It's been a long time, but I can still remember the picture of the putative Savior: a broad, strong-featured face under coarse, curling black hair, the sort of face that naturally belongs to a short, stocky man with broad hands and feet. Eyes large and black under heavy brows; mouth wide and full-lipped; beard heavy; neck thick; nose broad and short, with well-defined nostrils. Expression: direct, passionate, unsmiling, uncompromising. Not a figure we'd be apt to claim as Lord these days; more likely a person to get into trouble with the federal authorities. He looks a little too much like a potential terrorist.

This man couldn't have been further from the Jesus in the stained-glass windows of my church: the slender, elegant figure with the lanky light-brown hair and the gentle expression. Even Ralph Kozak's famous Laughing Jesus—a Jesus with his head thrown back, mouth wide open, laughing aloud—has the narrow, high-bridged nose that we tend to associate with aristocracy. The notion that Jesus might have looked like a working-class Palestinian is, however we cut it, more than a bit shocking.

But the image fits better with the Jesus I hear in the Gospels, a Jesus who may be riddling, demanding, unnerving, enigmatic, impossible, impassioned, exhausted, agonized, even sometimes wrong—but who is never, ever *respectable*. The Jesus of our stained glass windows might belong with the white middle class in Victorian times (that being when our church windows were made), but he'd be completely out of place among the poor of that or any other time. It's not that he would have rejected them, so much as they wouldn't have sought him out. The poor know perfectly well when they're in the company of people who'd rather they weren't.

No matter how hard we try to co-opt Jesus and turn him into our kind of guy, he remains stubbornly *other*. As a human being, he is Other: he belongs among the poor of perhaps the most troubled patch of land on God's green earth. Yet he also belongs among those who can play Torah the way Itzhak Perlman plays the fiddle; he is every inch a passionate Jew—but not a respectable one. No, never respectable.

That's just Jesus-as-man. What about Jesus-as-God?

When I pray "Christ have mercy," *Christe eleison,* I am praying to a scandalous figure. I am praying to a person who would be certainly pulled out of line at the airport and taken into a small room to be questioned by the authorities, if for no other reason than the expression in his eyes. I am praying to someone who could, quite plausibly, stride through the local shopping center with a club, bashing in the plate glass windows and bellowing to the shoppers to wise up to who their real gods are. I am praying to someone who took on unimaginable agony and sweated through it, who kept silence and stared at his tormentors with those huge, brilliant black eyes, his mother's eyes, driving them mad with frustrated rage. I am praying to someone who looked the lowliest in the face and loved them, not for anything they were or could do, but simply because they *were*: children of God, and therefore beloved.

Not a "Jesus, meek and mild." No, I don't think so.

But I can imagine those broad, short-fingered hands as being full of energy: stabbing a finger into a weathered, hardened palm to make a point, handling a carpenter's bit or a lamb with the sure calm of authority. I can imagine a small child sitting securely on that sturdy, brown, black-haired forearm, a brown dimpled starfish hand on his rounded, muscular shoulder. I can imagine him walking enormous distances with a strong stride. I can imagine him exhausted by the effort to heal everyone who needed healing—so many among his own people, and then there were all the others.

I can imagine him being harsh and exasperated, as he so often is in the Gospel. I can imagine him being really, *really* angry. But I can also imagine him with the sort of stubborn patience that outloves what drives you crazy, and with a deep, patient gentleness that surprises, but then makes excellent sense.

I can imagine him sleeping, exhausted and utterly relaxed. I know this sounds scandalous too, but it's in the Gospel: Jesus slept as the boat in which he was crossing the Sea of Galilee got into stormy waters. I can imagine him in the discipline of fasting, and also in the joy of a feast.

I can imagine him in the intimacy of close friendships—reaching out to grab Martha's wrist as she's scurrying to get dinner on the table, and pulling her gently down to rest. I can also imagine the terrible remoteness of being at once human and God, somewhere between the man who calls God *Abba* and the God who knows Godself. There's mystery here. We've tried for two millennia to plumb and understand this mystery, and understanding is not going to happen because it requires us to stretch beyond our own humanity and we can't do that. We can only wait for it all to be made plain to us.

I can imagine all this. I still understand that I must take this strange, demanding, impossible figure and somehow make him mine—my own personal Messiah at this beginning of a new millennium. This is what we've been doing in every single century since the Resurrection: trying to figure out not only who this person is, but also what he means; and the answers we come up with depend very much on who we are and when and where we are. It's a struggle.

Maybe for some lucky people, there's a single knock-you-off-your-donkey moment in which they encounter Christ, and that's it. I'm mildly jealous. For others of us, it isn't so; it's an ongoing process. For whatever God-given reason, I seem to have to keep wrestling with this Christ-stuff, struggling, reading, learning, giving up a cherished notion, trying again. It is the point and purpose of my life.

But I like to go back to the beginning point, to the scandalous figure who comes into the world (as his mother crowed at his conception) "turning the mighty from their seats and exalting the humble and meek." I like to imagine what it would be like to walk with him. Just for a moment, at least, before I have to turn back to this life I lead in this city, in this hour, in this life.

Be with me, Jesus, and keep me—not just in the safety of your saving grace, but in the fire of imagination and the boldness of proclamation. Maybe it's not an easy place to be, but when did you ever choose the safe way?

🎔 Kyrie Eleison (2) 🎔

Normally, the picture hangs on a wall in the living room, but I have taken it down and set it next to my computer so that I can tell you about it. It shows three winged figures seated around a cloth-covered table, upon which there sits a cup with food in it.

The figures—androgynous, graceful, both formal and intimate—look extremely ancient even though, in fact, the picture was painted in the fifteenth century. But it's Russian, and that makes all the difference. It is an icon, not a conventional painting.

The artist, Andrei Rublev, was ostensibly painting the three angels who came to tell Abram and Sarai about their impending conception of Isaac. But that doesn't fool anyone. It's known universally as the Rublev Trinity.

What's so powerfully fetching about this particular icon? The colors are surprisingly warm and gentle (if the reproduction I own is anything close to the truth). But that's not it. What shines from the image is a spirit of gentleness and deep intimacy. These three are *close*. Their faces express not glory or majesty, but vulnerability, trust, an almost childlike openness. Their heads are bent as they attend to each other intently, but they seem to have no need to speak. The closeness goes too deep for that.

It is the deep, loving, utterly safe intimacy that every healthy human being longs for with all his or her heart, and so few of us actually find. It is not love, but Love.

Father, Son, and Holy Spirit. Both a unitary God and a God who exists in community with Godself—a God who wants above all to be accepted as a lover, in the deep soul intimacy that lovers promise each other and sometimes partially fulfill.

My guess, and it's only a guess, is that God tried various ways of relating to us and found them unsatisfactory. Try to control us for our own good, and we just go off the rails. Try to win us through majesty and power, and we respond by finding more approachable little gods and idols. But even in the Old Testament, when humankind and God are constantly struggling toward some sort of accommodation, there are hints of this intimacy, of God's longing for us. "I led them with cords of human kindness, with bands of love. I was to them like those who lift infants to their cheeks," Hosea sings (11:4). "I bent down to them and fed them."

These three, seated around their table, are definitely beings who would lift infants to their cheeks and would delight in doing so.

I don't know (nobody is quite certain) which figure is supposed to be God the Father and which is supposed to be God the Son; the two are bending toward one another in tender attention. The figure to the right seems to be more inward-looking, still attentive, but thoughtful.

I look at this Person and remember the times that words have flowed through my fingers from God-knows-where, and I've known the truth of them, and I've also known the truth that I'm not responsible for them. I look at this Person and feel in myself the sense of *this way, not that way* or *this choice, not that,* coming not from my head but up through the soles of my feet. This is the God who sits with us in discernment, who abides with us as we struggle with beliefs and choices. This is the Comforter, who is sometimes so very uncomfortable.

This is the God who comes to dwell within us, to be so much a part of us that we're no longer obeying Big Daddy but instead shaping our lives from an inner sense of truth. Such a huge change; how can we take it so completely for granted?

This is also the God who has the power to move human beings in the here and now to pursue the Kingdom Way, if they choose to listen. There may be gentleness and intimacy in this thoughtful Spirit, but what about the power? Christians use wind as the metaphor for the Spirit's work, but I prefer the image of water, so subtle, so powerful, so taken-for-granted-universal, and so fundamental. I am at least 80 percent water, after all, and it is so intimately bound to the rest of me that I would die very quickly without it. I live near enough to big water to have some sense of its majesty and power, and the profound influence it has upon my landscape. This figure may be gentle, but it holds an authority to which I must respond, if I'm to heal and flourish.

One other thing about the picture: the three figures sit on three sides of the table. There is a fourth side, and it is open.

Child, come and be welcome. Come to the banquet.

I know I have no need for fear. None whatsoever, for I'll rest in these persons' arms and know what closeness really means, and I will learn to love as I am loved—if not now, then in the life to come.

> *May God be gracious unto us*
> *and bless us,*
> *and make his face to shine upon us,*
> *that your way may be known upon earth,*
> *your saving power among all nations.*
> *Let the peoples praise you, O God;*
> *let all the peoples praise you.*
>
> —PSALM 67:1–3

References

Anglican Church of Canada. *The Book of Alternative Services of the Anglican Church of Canada.* Toronto: Anglican Book Centre, 1985.

Caelius Sedulis, quoted in Warner, M. *Alone of All Her Sex: The Myth and Cult of the Virgin Mary.* London: Picador, 1995, xvii.

Campion, T. "Never Weather-Beaten Saile." In P. Vivian (ed.), *Campion's Works.* Oxford, England: Clarendon, 1909. I have modernized spelling in this poem and in the poems by Sidney (Chapter Three) and Southwell (Chapter Two).

Davies, R. *Tempest Tost.* Markham, Ont.: Penguin, 1987. For a description of the cathedral, see p. 10.

Donne, J. "A Valediction: Forbidding Mourning." In H. Kenner (ed.), *Seventeenth Century Poetry: The Schools of Donne and Jonson.* Austin, Tex.: Holt, Rinehart and Winston, 1967.

Goudge, E. *The Dean's Watch.* New York: Coward-McCann, 1960. For the passage on despair, see p. 126.

Holy Bible. New Revised Standard Version. Nashville, Tenn.: Nelson, 1989.

Lewis, C. S. *The Screwtape Letters.* London: Fount, 1977, Letter XV.

Lewis, C. S. *The Great Divorce.* San Francisco: Harper San Francisco, 2001. For the diamond-hard grass, see p. 25; for the backwash of glory, see p. 69.

Masterton, W. L., and Slowinski, E. J. *Chemical Principles Using the International System of Units.* Philadelphia: Saunders, 1977. The text in question is found on p. 52.

Peck, M. S. *The Road Less Traveled: A New Psychology of Love, Traditional Values, and Spiritual Growth.* New York: Simon & Schuster, 1978.

Robinson, S. "Praise the Lord and Pass the Ammunition." *Globe and Mail,* May 6, 2002, p. A17.

Sidney, P. "My True Love Hath My Heart and I Have His." In A. Feuillerat (ed.), *Sir Philip Sidney: The Last Part of the Countesse of Pembrokes Arcadia, Astrophel & Stella and Other Poems.* Cambridge, England: Cambridge University Press, 1922.

Smith, M. "The Original Abba," *Nativities and Passions.* Boston: Cowley, 1995.

Southwell, R. "Behold, a Silly Tender Babe." In B. Britten (comp.), *A Ceremony of Carols.* London: Hyperion Records, 1986.

Steed, J. *Our Little Secret: Confronting Child Sexual Abuse in Canada.* Toronto: Vintage Canada, 1995.

Thérèse of Liseaux, quoted in Peck, M. S. *People of the Lie.* New York: Simon and Schuster, 1983, p. 72.

Wilbur, R. "The Christmas Hymn." In *Advice to the Prophet and Other Poems.* Orlando: Harcourt Brace, 1961.

Yeats, W. B. "The Circus Animals' Desertion." In *Poems.* New York: Scribner, 1997.

The Author

Molly Wolf is a writer and editor living in Kingston, Ontario, with her two adult sons, Ross and John Greenough, and three cats, Magnificat (aka Maggie) and Calvin and Hobbes. Born in Illinois and raised there and in Vermont, she moved to Canada in 1971 and has lived in Nova Scotia and southeastern Ontario. She began writing short weekly essays (called Sabbath Blessings) in what she calls "kitchen table spirituality" in 1995 and has had three collections of her essays published. She is a mad, if not expert, knitter, who, with Linda Roghaar, coedits the *KnitLit* series (published by Three Rivers). She loves to cook, has a slightly overactive sense of humor, and sings tenor reasonably well. She knows a thing or two about Interesting Times. Other than that, she can't think of any biographical stuff, and besides, all the really important stuff is in the book.

A Hidden Wholeness:
The Journey Toward an Undivided Life
Parker J. Palmer
Hardcover
ISBN: 0–7879–7100–6

A BookSense Pick, September 2004

"This book is a treasure—an inspiring, useful blueprint for building safe places where people can commit to 'act in every situation in ways that honor the soul.'"

—*Publishers Weekly*

"The soul is generous: it takes in the needs of the world. The soul is wise: it suffers without shutting down. The soul is hopeful: it engages the world in ways that keep opening our hearts. The soul is creative: it finds its way between realities that might defeat us and fantasies that are mere escapes. All we need to do is to bring down the wall that separates us from our own souls and deprives the world of the soul's regenerative powers."

—From *A Hidden Wholeness*

At a time when many of us seek ways of working and living that are more resonant with our souls, *A Hidden Wholeness* offers insight into our condition and guidance for finding what we seek—within ourselves and with each other.

Parker J. Palmer is a highly respected writer, lecturer, teacher, and activist. Author of six previous books—including the best-sellers *Let Your Life Speak* and *The Courage to Teach*—he has been recognized with eight honorary doctorates and his writing has won several national awards. He holds a Ph.D. from the University of California at Berkeley and lives in Madison, Wisconsin.

Finding Our Way Home:
Turning Back to What Matters Most
Mark R. McMinn
Hardcover
ISBN: 0–7879–7531–1

"In some quarters, Christians have a reputation for being deathly afraid of diversity, conflict, humor, sexuality, and most of the other things that help make life worth living. Here is a book to prove it need not be so. Mark R. McMinn writes honestly, movingly, and well from his rich immersion in life, exploring experiences we can all identify with and finding the dimension of depth hidden in them. He helps us to understand the enlivening and liberating meaning of 'the Word became flesh and dwelt among us, full of grace and truth.'"
—Parker J. Palmer, author of *A Hidden Wholeness, Let Your Life Speak,* and *The Courage to Teach.*

"We are all caught within the confusing and contradictory swirl of emotions like love and hate, hope and despair, remembering and forgetfulness, loathing and longing. Mark R. McMinn pointedly reveals that what so ruthlessly and lovingly draws them all together is the deep gravitational pull of home."
—Michael Card, musician and author, *A Fragile Stone* and *Scribbling in the Sand*

Mark R. McMinn (Winfield, Illinois) is the Dr. Arthur P. Rech and Mrs. Jean May Rech Professor of Psychology at Wheaton College, where he also initiated and directs the Center for Church-Psychology Collaboration. He has authored over one hundred journal articles and chapters, as well as seven books, including *Why Sin Matters.*